party LIKE it's 2044

party LIKE it's 2044

Finding the Funny

in Life and Death

Joni B. Cole

University of New Mexico Press   Albuquerque

Library of Congress Cataloging-in-Publication Data

ISBN 978-0-8263-6556-9 (paper)

ISBN 978-0-8263-6557-6 (electronic)

Library of Congress Control Number: 2023937363

Founded in 1889, the University of New Mexico sits
on the traditional homelands of the Pueblo of Sandia.
The original peoples of New Mexico—Pueblo, Navajo,
and Apache—since time immemorial have deep
connections to the land and have made significant
contributions to the broader community statewide.
We honor the land itself and those who remain
stewards of this land throughout the generations
and also acknowledge our committed relationship
to Indigenous peoples. We gratefully recognize our
history.

The essays "Winning Women" and "But Enough about
Me" were originally published in *Another Bad-Dog
Book: Essays on Love, Life, and Neurotic Human Behavior*
and have been slightly revised for this collection.

*To protect the innocent, lots of identifying details have been
changed, but not the truth. (Or at least my truth.) Also, as
several of these essays reflect, sometimes my imagination
informs my reality, but it's still my reality, for better or worse.*

Cover photograph adapted from image by Isabella
Fischer on unsplash.com
Cover design by Isaac Morris
Illustrations by Helmut Baer
Designed by Isaac Morris
Composed in Ayuthaya, Bona Nova, and Reross

To Helmut Baer. (Please read the essay that starts on page 76. And if I ever seem to forget why you're the perfect boyfriend for me, remind me to also read that essay.)

Contents

We'll Never Have Guatemala

Yet again, the conversation turns to Guatemala.

My boyfriend, Helmut, and I are hosting a little dinner party with four friends. We're seated around the dining table in my condo, located in a small town in Vermont that is 3,559 miles from Guatemala, eating food that has nothing to do with Guatemala, previously discussing some obscure jazz musician I've never heard about but am pretty sure never toured in Guatemala. And yet.

"We're thinking about going back to Guatemala next winter," one of our guests, a retired linguist, announces out of nowhere. His wife, a musician, adds, "It's so beautiful there, and flights are unbelievably cheap."

"I love Guatemala!" enthuses the yoga instructor seated across from me. "Did you know it has thirty-seven active volcanoes?"

"The Guatemalan people are so friendly," the yoga instructor's date chimes in, instantly earning a strike against him. Oh, come on, I think. How can every single person in a country be friendly? Surely there is at least one curmudgeon in the bunch.

Helmut knows enough to keep his mouth shut. Not because he hasn't been to Guatemala—he has, twice—but because he knows this is pretty much the only thing I don't like about him after nine years of togetherness. When Helmut was in his twenties, long before I met him, he left his home in the Black Forest in Germany and traveled extensively, at one point landing in San Cristobal, Mexico. There he met some

1

random young American woman who told him he just had to go to Guatemala.

"It's the most amazing place," she'd exclaimed, probably after they'd had sex, though Helmut never shared this level of detail with me. Regardless, this young American woman clearly had no concern for Helmut's well-being, or for my need decades later to snag him for a post-divorce, midlife romance. Never mind that Guatemala was experiencing a brutal civil war at the time. Never mind that on the bus Helmut took to Panajachel in the Guatemalan Highlands, gangs of vigilantes body-searched the passengers at regular checkpoints to make sure none of them were guerillas posing as civilians. For all I know, Helmut was a guerilla back then, so one day I asked him what exactly he wanted to do in Guatemala.

"Play guitar," he'd answered.

In the middle of a civil war?! In a town with a marketplace where the storefronts were riddled with bullet holes?! If I was his mother back in the Black Forest, I would have killed him.

Here, I want to share for the record that I have nothing personal against Guatemala. In fact, just the opposite. As a first-world homebody who has never traveled there or much of anywhere, I know the country mostly through the lens of headlines about migration and poverty. But I also know that Guatemala's geography is stunningly beautiful, the country enjoys a thriving tourist industry, and its capital is a hub for entrepreneurs. ("You remember our neighbor's son, Roy," said the retired linguist at our dinner table. "Now he's running a tech start-up in Guatemala City, and it's really taking off!")

I am happy for Roy. Truly. And I am hopeful for Guatemala, even as this small Central American country, where almost half its population are descendants of the ancient Mayans, continues to suffer the horrors of gang-related violence and other challenges. Similar to how I feel about all the troubled spots in the world, I just want everyone there to be happy and safe, but if that can't happen, then I want the people there to come here and feel happy and safe. Goodness knows, given the polarized state of America, we could certainly use an influx of an entire country of friendly people.

No, my problem isn't with the country of Guatemala per se, but rather how all my friends (and their neighbors, and their neighbor's children) seem to have spent time there and feel compelled to rave about the place at my table. Maybe this is an example of frequency illusion. Once Helmut told me about his Guatemalan adventures—inadvertently making me feel like I had misspent my own young adulthood as a shut-in—Guatemala seemed to pop up in every conversation. Or maybe it's an example of confirmation bias, where I have become so sensitized to the subject that now I recall conversations in a way that simply affirms my belief that I am the only person in the world who has never traveled to this particular spot on the globe. Whatever the phenomenon, real or imagined, the result is that Guatemala has come to represent one of my most shameful secrets, which is this: I do not want to travel there. Indeed, I do not want to go much of anywhere, neither geographically nor in the realm of time travel, at least to any era before there were toilets.

It is embarrassing for me to admit that I am not an eager traveler, even to places where the marketplace is not riddled with bullet holes. Clearly, I was behind the door when God passed out the desire for passport stamps. Maybe this is not a problem for Italian nanas who came from the old country and—once resettled in their Italian neighborhoods in the Bronx—see no reason to learn English or venture much further than their savory-smelling kitchens. But in my social circles, several of which are occupied by folks with advanced degrees and a modicum of disposable income, my lack of wanderlust makes me feel like an outsider and an old fogy. *In my day, we didn't need to go anywhere. Now let me eat my dinner in peace because it's almost five o'clock.* This is why I am overly sensitive when the conversation gets global and why I go to lengths to hide my shameful secret. Some recent examples:

Over lunch the other day, a friend announced that he was moving to Taiwan for a year on a Fulbright Scholarship. "You should visit me while I'm there!" he said. "You'll have a free place to stay."

"The children," I shook my head sadly, as if my two daughters, both in their twenties, still need me at home to fix them macaroni and cheese.

"I want to take you to Germany." Helmut has made this generous offer countless times in the past. "My mom would love to meet you." The woman lived to be 101, but I always found an excuse.

My best cover though, is the way I have encouraged my kids to travel, which provides the perfect deflection. "Go! Go!" My urgings have supported their participation in programs that have allowed them to walk the Inca Trail to Machu Picchu, build toilets in Nicaragua, cavort with ancient tortoises in the Galápagos Islands . . . It is like I have Munchausen's by proxy, only the travel version in which I, the caregiver, garner positive attention for myself by foisting travel adventures on my daughters.

The talk around my dining table has now turned to food, and because it is clearly impossible to exhaust the topic of Guatemala, the conversation loiters around food experienced in that country.

"You can't get authentic chile rellenos in America, not like the ones they make in Guatemala."

"The best grilled *robalo* I ever ate was from a street vendor in Antigua."

Suddenly, these friends all sound like NPR commentators, pronouncing perfectly Americanized words with a Spanish affectation. I stand abruptly and start refilling wine glasses. The only languages I speak are English and crossword-puzzle Latin. Even worse, I really like the chile rellenos they serve at a café in Burlington, Vermont, which is in America the last time I looked.

"I'm going to Montana!" I announce. The relief! To have this one travel talking point of my own outweighs any self-consciousness about abruptly changing the subject. "I'm going for two weeks in the spring." The trip is still months away, but already I have made my travel arrangements, partly because I am organized, but mostly for accountability. Now that I have paid good money for an airline ticket, I know that I won't back out.

"Why Montana?" My friends, good-natured to a one, easily shift their attention to this new topic, and to me.

In my mind's eye I see a vast night sky, a blackish-purple canopy fractured by a flash of forked lightning. The image became imprinted on my mind over twenty-five years ago, after my former husband and I took a rare vacation out West. We were in some remote town, standing outside during a rainless storm. When the lightning split open the sky, it felt like I was glimpsing the great beyond. I have long wanted to return to that sky, to relive that sense of mystery and awe.

Why Montana? I hesitate before answering. "It's such a beautiful place," I say. "I've wanted to go back there for years." I don't mention the specific memory that prompted my travel plans because, truth be told, I am not even sure I was in Montana at the time I witnessed that storm. The geography of those western states is fuzzy in my mind, and the landscape I recall looked a lot like the setting for my favorite Netflix series, *Longmire*, about a taciturn sheriff in Absaroka County. The problem is, Absaroka County is in Wyoming.

"We're renting a house in Bozeman," I add. "I found it through a friend of a friend." I tell everyone about my email exchanges with the homeowner, who lives locally but has this second house across the country. When I had written to her asking about availability and cost, the woman responded with a friendly message that didn't answer my questions, but did include a photo of her kitchen sink, "found on the side of the road, and with a $450 faucet!"

I have never been a student of fixtures—they just seem to come with the homes where I have lived—so I had no idea if the mention of a $450 faucet was intended as an apology (Beware, the place is a dump!) or a promise of luxury and a precursor to proffering an exorbitant rental price. (We charge $5,000 a week, and a Keurig is not included!) As it turns out, a Keurig does not come with the house, but the amount the woman and her husband were asking was more than a fair price, and if caffeine became an issue, she assured me I would be able to walk to a nearby café.

At my dining table, the conversation moves on to other topics, mercifully not travel-related, but I continue to ponder the question: Why Montana? It does seem odd that a state renowned for its conservative politics and its strong gun culture would have such a strong pull for someone like me, a liberal who believes, as countless bumper stickers in Vermont can attest, that arms are for hugging. As our gathering winds down, I finish my dinner, grateful for the delicious meal that Helmut has prepared and the good fortune of having these friends with whom to enjoy it. Yet even now, I feel an urge to experience another reality, something beyond these everyday blessings right in front of me at this table.

Why Montana? Maybe I am putting way too much stock in a distant memory. Or maybe Montana will be my Guatemala.

After our friends leave, I sit at my computer and reread emails from the woman whose second home we will be renting in Bozeman. In one, she describes the house as "quirky but comfortable." In another, she tells me about the fun she and her husband have riding bikes and cross-country skiing in West Yellowstone. She expresses relief that I don't want to rent their house until late spring, after which she will be able to see to the place rather than her husband who is currently there for work. "I was a little worried about my husband having to set up the house for your visit," she wrote. "What if he put the peach sheets on the beds in the yellow room? :)."

At the end of her most recent email she writes, "I'm looking forward to meeting and handing you the keys."

I shut down the computer and head to bed. For a nontraveler like me, two weeks spent across the country feels like a long time to be away from my life; away from my own quirky but comfortable home. I wonder, will Montana change me? At the least, I suppose, it will help me stop confusing it with Wyoming. Maybe it will help me understand gun culture. It might even give me a greater appreciation of faucets.

Helmut is outside, having a nightcap on our small patio. He often checks out the stars before calling it a night. I try to imagine what goes through his head as he looks at the sky above our little patch of the universe. Is he filled with that sense of mystery and awe that I experienced all those years ago during that rainless storm? Is he thinking about our life together and how lucky he is to live here with me? Or maybe he is feeling regret that he has chosen a partner who doesn't share his love of travel, his sense of adventure.

We'll never have Guatemala, I think, feeling my own sense of regret. The line is a riff, of course, from the closing scene of *Casablanca*, when the two former lovers, Rick and Ilsa, are about to part forever. "We'll always have Paris," Rick tells Ilsa, referring to their brief romance in Paris on the eve of World War II. What he means is that they'll always be together in those shared memories of that special time and place. But Helmut and I don't have a Paris, or much worse, we don't have a Guatemala.

As I wait for Helmut to come to bed, I burrow beneath my comforter and conjure up the memory of that forked lightning, as bright as a billion volts of electricity. A worry crosses my mind: What if I get hit by lightning when I am in Montana? It could happen, I think, with a sky that big. On the other hand, Montana may not be as enticing as a place with thirty-seven active volcanoes, or authentic chile rellenos, or an entire population of friendly people, but if it comes with a shock of electricity, at least metaphorically speaking, maybe that's just the kind of jolt that I need.

The Other Woman

"Not everyone is equipped to work well with people." Truer words, but I never expected anyone to think such a thing about me. Yet those are the exact words shared by a disgruntled former writing client who has written me a single-spaced, three-page letter explaining why she cannot, in good conscience, recommend my services should anyone ask.

Really? I toss the letter on my kitchen counter. I am not equipped to work well with people? I beg to differ. I have taught hundreds of writing students—people who take my workshops again and again or work with me individually, often for the duration of their projects. Many of these people have become good friends. Indeed, in twenty-plus years of teaching I have received lots and lots of thank-yous, lauding me for my insights, my positive attitude, my encouragement and support. Many of these appreciations I have kept in a sunny yellow folder on the bottom shelf of my bookcase. The folder is labeled "Nice Things People Have Said about Me."

The signature on the letter is a name I don't recognize—a name I have changed in this essay to Donna, inspired by a girl I knew in middle school who also made me feel bad about myself but for totally different reasons. (*No, middle-school Donna, I cannot do a split, and thank you for pointing that out during cheerleading tryouts.*)

But who is this letter-writing Donna who feels the need to disparage me as both a teacher and human being? Just listen to this nonsense she spouts on the page—"I value constructive feedback from an expert. This is not about the thickness of my skin. Rather, it's about the self-awareness, empathy, and social skills that contribute to one's emotional intelligence, and your seeming lack thereof."

Really, Donna? *Thereof*?

I Google Donna's name but nothing pops up. Right there, it seems that should disqualify her from judging me. Maybe she is just a private person, but on the other hand you would think her name would at least be in the minutes of some PTA meeting or public works committee. *In attendance: Donna* . . . Oh wait, strike that. Clearly our Donna has no problem ignoring her civic duties so that she can stay at home to compose hate mail.

The letter had been enclosed in a sealed envelope with no postage, only my name—Joni B. Cole—handwritten on it. My friend, Frances, with whom I occasionally share an office where I teach writing workshops and where she practices New Age healing, had dropped it off at my house while I was out doing errands. On the outside of the envelope Frances had stuck a Post-it Note—*This is for you. Have a beautiful day!* As is her habit, she had signed the note with a heart. Because the letter, weirdly enough, bore a date from over a year ago, I assumed it had been accidentally mixed in with Frances's client notes or divination cards, and she had only recently come across it. Likely, she thought she was doing me a favor, delivering it to my house with a sweet Post-it.

I reread the pages once more, then stuff them back in their envelope, my fingers already anticipating the satisfaction of shoving Donna and her low opinion of me in the trash. This is my usual MO whenever I receive an unpleasant communication on paper or online. Who needs all those rejection letters from editors polluting my inbox with their negative energy? *Doesn't meet our needs . . . Didn't pique our interest . . . Before submitting, we recommend you subscribe to our publication* . . . Delete! Delete! Don't bet on it!

Then I change my mind for one particular reason. In the letter, Donna references one of my books for aspiring authors, in which I include what she describes as a "mean" story about a former workshop participant. "Such vitriol," Donna writes, "for someone who paid you good money to help, not hurt." Hold on there, I think. Donna had missed the entire point of that story, which ultimately demonstrated how the workshop participant had overcome her defensiveness and learned to listen to feedback and effectively apply it. But now it seems Donna is using that story as context for delivering a not-so-veiled warning—*Don't even think about writing about me in one of your little books.*

Ha! Dream on, honey. If I had not already been thinking about Donna as material for a future essay or chapter, I certainly was now. No one has the right to tell me what I can and cannot write, give or take a few libel laws. Which meant Donna's letter was no longer simply deserving of the garbage can; now it was opposition research.

In war, there exists the concept of the Other. The Other is the enemy, a homologous force that threatens your beliefs, your way of life, your liberties. A soldier's training often incorporates imagery of the Other, for example shooting at targets outfitted in helmets bearing a Soviet red star or an American flag, depending on the war and whose side you are on. In this way, soldiers are conditioned to view the enemy as an abstraction, a faceless threat, a symbol rather than an individual or fellow human being.

Of course, the concept of the Other extends well beyond war. In religion, one of the hardest things for the faithful to do is to not just tolerate the Other but to love them, without any need to convert them. In politics, as well, one party often capitalizes on the fear of the Other, an unfortunate but usually effective method of campaigning. In life in general, the Other can be defined through myriad perspectives, creating all sorts of fault lines between people with opposing views and different lifestyles. Take, for example, Prius owners, their car being the epitome of the Other for drivers of gas guzzlers who actually have someplace they need to be on their twenty miles per gallon.

As a Prius driver myself, I know what it feels like to be categorically vilified. For this reason, among many more, I like to think I am too evolved a human being to succumb to such divisive conditioning and generalized hate. If I am going to dislike someone, it will be on a case-by-case basis, and not just because that person's hybrid (MPG: 58 city/53 highway) represents some existential threat to their predilection for fossil fuels. All this to say, never in a million years would I have guessed that I, too, could harbor hostility across a wide swath of humanity. I did not have an Other. Or so I thought, until Donna's letter arrived on my kitchen counter.

In truth, I would have loved to forget all about Donna and her low opinion of me, yet in the weeks after its arrival I found myself returning to her neatly typed and grammatically anal letter again and again, like a dog working a rawhide even after its gums are bloodied. In addition to her disdain for me, those three single-spaced pages illuminated something else about this woman, which is that either Donna had an echoic memory or had missed her calling as a court reporter.

Like a meticulously prepared prosecution, she starts her argument by replaying our very first phone conversation. In this early November call, Donna recounts how she had asked me if I wanted to delay our meeting until after Thanksgiving, given the busy time of year.

"No need to wait," I had told her. In my hazy recollection of this initial exchange, I remember thinking, here is an anxious writer, already getting cold feet about sharing her work, and of course part of my job is to help writers overcome that fear by not giving them an out. "This is what I do for a living," I had added, aiming for reassurance. But to Donna's ear, my tone implied, *What a silly question. I'm already looking down on you.*

Donna also took issue with how I behaved during the meeting, which took place at a coffee shop where I often consult with clients. "You looked up at nearly every person who walked by, which left me feeling like your focus was divided."

Most notably, her letter devotes several paragraphs to my feedback on a particular scene in her essay in which the narrator (Donna) is in her backyard, hanging laundry on a clothesline. Hers is a suburban neighborhood, and in that scene she describes how, as she is enjoying this household chore, she hears birds and a nearby lawn mower.

When I critiqued Donna's work, I had written in the margin next to that scene—"I'm not buying this." During our meeting, she asked me to clarify that comment, so I told her that I did not think it possible to hear birds over a running lawn mower. To this Donna responds in her letter, "You made me feel as though you had questioned the honesty in my writing. I felt you had not read my words here as carefully as you should have, and I didn't appreciate the glib insinuation."

Her letter goes on to document several more of my transgressions. Here, I was "negative." There, I "muttered to myself." Donna even finds fault with my handwriting, "The edits aren't helpful if the writer can't read them."

I stick the letter in my bookcase, hidden underneath my sunny yellow folder full of nice things people have said about me. Unfortunately, however, out of sight does not always mean out of mind, and in the days that follow I find myself refuting her criticisms.

I do not lack social skills!

I do too have emotional intelligence!

I'm not even sure what "glib" means!

Still, my thoughts keep coming back to that scene in her essay, the one where Donna is in her backyard, hanging her family's laundry. Of all the things I had forgotten about that single encounter with Donna—her name, her face, and most of the particulars of her story—I did remember that scene, even without her prompting.

My mind recreates those paragraphs. There Donna is, standing in her suburban backyard. A basket of wet clothes rests at her feet. Birds are singing, which, miraculously, she can hear above the roar of a nearby lawn mower. The scene fades to black, but what lingers in my mind, in vivid relief, is the image of that clothesline, a symbol of domesticity. More specifically, to me the clothesline is a symbol of *uber* domesticity, in which women happily eschew dryers and do other things that I could never see myself doing, like reheating leftovers in the oven instead of the microwave, or making crackers from scratch, or engaging in craftivism by lending their domestic arts to the fight for social justice. In my psyche, Donna's clothesline is as powerful a symbol as the American flag or a Soviet red star on a helmet. It triggers a conditioned response—This is the enemy, a threat to my self-esteem, my liberties, my way of life.

That is when it hits me with a flash of clarity. Donna is not just a disgruntled writing client armed with a pocketful of clothespins. Donna is my Other.

Of course, I was not cognizant of this conditioned response in me when I first read Donna's manuscript or when I sat across from her in that bustling coffeeshop. Contrary to some people's opinions, I do have professional standards and a degree of decorum. Plus, I doubt if it was even possible to look up at nearly everyone who walked by our table. Yet now I could understand why Donna had read insensitivity, even negativity into my words and actions.

"I'm not buying this." That is the comment I had scribbled in the margin next to the scene with the clothesline.

Translation: "I am sorry, Donna, if you and all those other uber-domestic types just like you are too good for dryers. But I believe in dryers! And no outsider is going to make me feel bad for using one. And just for the record, I also believe in dryer sheets! So don't go telling me they're toxic and full of chemicals that will elevate my estrogen levels. Newsflash, Donna, I wouldn't mind a little more estrogen. Plus, dryer sheets smell more like the outdoors than the real outdoors, at least if you get the scented kind."

To ease my worries that Donna might be totally right about me, I show her letter to a few friends, all of whom have my back.

"What a wacko!"

"Why do you care what that woman thinks?"

"You're the last person I'd describe as mean!"

"I'm sorry I ever brought that letter into your house," says Frances. The sweet Post-it Note she had attached to the envelope is long gone, lost in all my retrieving and returning of the letter to my bookcase.

"Where did you find it anyway?" I ask her, picturing Donna's missive hiding behind some papers on Frances's desk, all the while accruing more evidence of my failings as it watches me lead my writing workshops.

"I didn't find it anywhere," Frances says. "Someone slid it under our door the day that I brought it to you."

Well now. This adds a whole new twist. Maybe Donna really is a wacko because what kind of person takes this long to write a letter about a relatively brief encounter that happened over a year ago? Or maybe—an image forms in my mind—maybe Donna spent all those months stewing and revising, stewing and revising, wanting to get her word choice just right. (*Should I phrase it—Not everyone is* equipped *to work well with people . . . Or would it be stronger if I wrote—Not everyone is* able *to work well with people?*) This image of Donna maniacally editing makes it easier to discount her, to have some fun at her expense. That and her use of the word "thereof."

I peruse the letter one last time, lingering on a particular passage near the end. "At one point," Donna adds, "I told you that I had begun to take my writing more seriously, whereas I used to consider it more of a hobby, sometimes feeling guilty about working on it the way I might when taking time out to knit. It was a casual, incomplete comment, to which you reacted with a face that spoke volumes, and not in a good way."

Ah, that face. That face has been my undoing since forever, but especially when I was a teenager. Mine was a mother you did not cross. You did not talk back. You did not consciously or unconsciously roll your eyes. Yet, despite my best efforts to appear neutral, I always seemed to give myself away.

"Get that look off your face" was one of my mother's most frequent refrains.

"What look? I don't look like anything!" I would proclaim my innocence. And yet there were my true feelings on display, as prominent as the acne on my forehead.

Of course Donna had been able to read between my lines. Of course she had picked up on what I had failed to recognize or acknowledge even to myself. Her letter made it apparent: it is not possible to fully hide your dislike of the Other, any more than you can fool your mother or hear birds over a running lawnmower.

I tuck Donna's letter back in its envelope and return it to my bookshelf, where it can continue to do battle with my sunny folder full of nice things people have said about me. Let my admirers tell Donna a thing or two! But if I am going to live up to their high praise of me as a writing teacher and human being, I will need to get over my conditioned response to clotheslines and other triggers. I will need to stop vilifying people who simply believe in uber-domesticity or enjoy a lifestyle remote from my own.

Yet, even in this moment of resolve, I recognize an undercurrent of hostility that I can no longer pretend is not there. Why was I not surprised to learn from Donna's letter that she is someone who takes time out to knit? Don't they all, I think, the whole nameless, faceless, threatening lot of them, those Other women who hang their family's clothes in the fresh air to dry and wield their knitting needles like enemy swords.

Our Old House

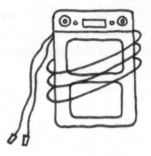

"I want to buy you a new oven," I tell my ex-husband, Steve, who still lives in the Vermont home we shared for over two decades. After our divorce several years ago, I moved to a condo a few minutes away, relieved to be done not only with the marriage but also with the responsibilities that came with maintaining our quirky and well-worn house.

"That's really nice," Steve says in response to my offer to replace this ailing appliance. "Let me think about it."

What is there to think about? Both units of his double oven have been on the fritz for at least two years. The meals our family has cooked at my ex's since the oven stopped working properly have become an exercise in emergency interventions. Every half hour, Steve has to open the door to ameliorate the oven's sudden temperature spikes, then close the door to raise the temperature above the wattage of a tanning bed, then open the door, then close the door, and so on and so on. Last Thanksgiving the roasted turkey looked like one of those octogenarian snowbirds who returns to Vermont from Florida with leathered skin but a fleshy underbelly.

"Well, let me know when you're done thinking," I say, feeling deflated. I often fantasize myself as the magnanimous gift giver and now, for once, I actually have some extra income thanks to the pandemic, which had been a boon to my online writing workshops but also made me feel like a profiteer. The least I can do is put the extra income to good use by assuring that my family doesn't die of salmonella poisoning. Unfortunately, like countless times during our marriage, my tendency toward impulsivity collides with Steve's habit of overthinking, and we find ourselves in a situation not unlike the malfunctioning oven's— faltering between too much and too little heat.

A week later, I raise the topic again. Despite the divorce, old habits die hard, like my badgering Steve to get my way, with his resistance only galvanizing my efforts and reinforcing my certainty that I know best.

"So, about that oven?" I figured it would run me about $2,500, which is burning a hole in my pocket. "It makes sense to replace it now," I say, "given that we can't sell the house without a working oven, and this way you can actually get some use out of it before you move." With both our girls recently out of college, Steve and I have started talking about the best timing for selling this house, allowing him to find a smaller place that is easier to maintain. I say "our" house because we still jointly own this property, but it is his home now.

Steve crosses the kitchen and opens the door to the upper oven. We both peer inside the dark, cold space. What is there to see but remains from our family life baked into the walls, evidence of countless home-cooked meals but also irreversible neglect.

"Well?" I nudge.

"Okay," he concedes, shutting the door. "But let me pay for it." This is also typical Steve, responsible and fair-minded. It may not have been his idea to replace the oven, but that doesn't mean he shouldn't pay for it, at least according to him. But that was not part of this deal.

"All you'll have to do is come home from work one day to a brand new oven," I say. Negotiation over, I hustle to the door.

"You know it probably won't be a simple replacement," Steve runs his hand through his salt-and-pepper hair. "I doubt if it conforms to a typical size." On that point, we can totally agree. In fact, few things associated with this house have lent themselves to simple repairs or easy answers.

The house started as a small, one-story dwelling built in the early 1800s, its few rooms encircling a central fireplace with three shallow hearths and a beehive oven. At times, our friends have remarked how they sensed ghosts in this old section of the house, but I am not so sure. After Steve and I decided to divorce, one of those original rooms became my bedroom, as we spent over a year hashing out the logistics of money, custody, and establishing two homes for the girls. I can't say I ever saw ghosts those nights I occupied this space, but sometimes I would sense a comingling of the past and present in the dust particles visible in the lamplight. *Detach with love*, I reminded myself, sleepless night after night, when my anger threatened our fragile coexistence.

While most of the original structure has remained intact, the house saw modest additions through the decades, that is until the early 1980s when the people who lived here prior to us decided to quadruple its size and add showy features. Unfortunately, however, before these same owners could cap the newly built stone walls, or close the gaping spaces between the refurbished pine floorboards, or rethink the preponderance of ugly, green wallpaper in the downstairs rooms, the recession hit. As a result, they lost this property to foreclosure, as well as another one down the road where, next to that home, they had built an octagonal hippodrome for their pet elephant.

In hindsight, maybe Steve and I should have been more wary of buying a house from people who thought of an elephant as a pet. On the other hand, we had been living in efficiency apartments for a decade, and this four-thou-sand-square-foot historical hybrid was a bank-owned property, meaning it was affordable even for us, a fledgling author and newly minted psychologist.

"It feels like a miracle," I remember saying to Steve on the first day we moved into the house. I saw plenty of cobwebs in the big empty rooms but no shadows lurking in the corners, no premonitory signs of trouble. We could sleep in a bed that did not double as a sofa. We could host dance parties in the wide-open living room. I could bake bread in the beehive oven, or at least brag that we had a fireplace with a beehive oven. And we could have babies who would grow up with memories of their perfect childhood in their perfect, cobwebby home.

Eight weeks after ordering the new double oven, I am in Steve's kitchen, watching a man sweating and grunting as he works to dislodge the old unit to make way for the new. As anticipated, the broken oven proved to be a nontraditional size, reducing the possibilities for replacement to one model that "might fit," according to a Best Buy appliance specialist. Please, please, please let this go smoothly, I silently prayed. The last thing I want is for Steve to come home to a brand new double oven sitting in the middle of his kitchen, next to a gaping hole in the wall. Courtesy of me.

Our old cat, Milo, brushes against my legs. Once a sleek Siamese, now he is scrawny and scarred from countless brawls with nocturnal critters. I stroke his bony head, remembering how Steve and I adopted him as a Christmas present for the girls when they were little. We tried to hide him in our bedroom until Christmas morning but they heard his mewling and coaxed him from under our bed. It seems impossible that Milo still exists, not just because he is an outdoor prowler, but because he seems like an anachronism of our life as a family before. Before the divorce. Before the kids grew up. Before we found a new normal.

"You got a problem," the installer hitches up his pants and shakes his head in my direction. I cross all my fingers that aren't gripping my coffee cup. He tries to explain to me the outdated features of the old oven's wiring and why he won't be able to hook up the new appliance. "Take a look," he insists, which is the last thing I want to do, but we squat side by side and peer into the space still partially occupied by the lower oven. I follow the beam of his flashlight to two ropey wires, one black, one red, that feed downward through the floor, presumably—from the ominous tone of the installer's voice—into the ninth circle of hell. "I'm gonna need to fetch some parts at the hardware store," he says.

While he is gone, I take advantage of his absence to roam the downstairs, revisiting rooms steeped in memories. It is nice to see familiar family photos displayed on the built-in shelves, on the triple mantles of the fireplace, on the walls. In the kitchen, I recall how the side of the long center island served as the "art gallery" where we taped the girls' countless drawings and paintings. The long floorboards, running from the front of the house to the back; this was the parade route where the girls lined up hundreds of their plastic farm animals and dinosaurs and Polly Pockets. In the backroom, my former makeshift bedroom, I listen for ghosts. Instead, I hear my own past self, whispering my mantra: *"Detach with love. Detach with love. Detach with love."*

The oven installer has been busy since his return from the hardware store. By now, he has removed the old appliance and clipped and sealed off the fat red and black wires that fed it electricity. To power the new oven, he also has created an electrical box that skirted the need for him to drill through the floor and take a sledgehammer to one of the basement walls. "Strain reliefs," he listed among the items he picked up at the hardware store. As a writer, I appreciate the metaphor.

"You're good to go," the installer finally announces. After he gathers his tools and rolls away the old oven on a hand truck, a familiar relief washes over me, reminiscent of conversations with so many service people past:

> From the fellow we hired to line the chimney with the three, shallow hearths: "It's going to take a lot of wet cement. There's a chance it could bring the whole thing down."

> From the contractor tasked with replacing our failed septic system: "Yup, just what I feared. You don't have any room in your lawn for another leach field."

> From the emergency plumber we summoned when a pipe burst inside the wall: "Problem is, it's going to be near impossible to get to that sucker."

Yet in those situations, just like now, ultimately a solution was found. Not unlike my relationship with Steve, I think. On the brink of hopelessness, we figured out how to make our relationship work, and all it took was the strain relief that came from our divorce.

After the installer leaves, I am reluctant to leave the comfort of Steve's kitchen. Milo is sleeping on the chair next to mine, while I stroke his bony back and listen to his raggedy purr. The shiny new oven keeps catching my eye, reminding me that one day soon we will sell this place. There was a time after the divorce when I could not even make the short drive from my condo back to this house without triggering feelings of anxiety and guilt. The regrets of our failed marriage, the weight of our big, old house, made me eager to say good riddance. Now, I am not so sure.

I have read how places hold onto energy—how the words, and feelings, and memories of the people who came before linger after they are gone. It makes me wonder, when the next family moves in, what will remain of us? Obviously, some walls covered in ugly green wallpaper that we never found the time or money to replace. Also, countless tape marks on the side of the kitchen island, plus an assortment of paper clips and hair ties forever lost to those gaps between the floorboards.

But what about emotions? What about all the love and joy we brought to this house, reflected in the family photos still on display? What about the anger of those last difficult years of our marriage that hung in the air like the dust illuminated in the lamplight of my makeshift bedroom? Will that negative energy also be part of our legacy?

The answer reveals itself in a glint of stainless steel. I imagine our next Thanksgiving a few months from now, in this kitchen, at this same table, where a perfectly roasted turkey is waiting to be carved. It feels like a miracle, I think, which I realize is the same thought I had when Steve and I first moved into this house over two decades ago. Those emotions—the bad ones that haunted this place during those last, painful years—are gone, exorcized from this home, just like the old double oven that threatened to do us in as a family but didn't quite get the chance.

Dear Mr. Impaler

Dear Mr. Impaler (Or do you prefer Mr. Vlad the Impaler. Or Dracula?),

First, please don't kill me. Second, I know how important and busy you are as an authoritarian leader with several personality disorders, but you are one of the most—I'm sorry, *the most*—(Please don't kill me!) qualified person to address the following question: Isn't it enough to vanquish your enemy? Do you really need to skewer them as well?

It seems to me it takes a good amount of exertion to be just normal, everyday cruel? Why do you feel compelled to go the extra mile—to bring captors from the villages you plunder back to your castle in Transylvania and then execute them by impalement? Even if a prisoner is of average size, impaling cannot be easy, given the required upper body strength. And all that whittling!

For years, I have been curious about you and your excessive cruelty. Rumor has it you like to dine among your impaled victims, dipping your bread in their blood. Of course I am not alone in my fascination. The author Bram Stoker must have seen dollar signs when he came across your name in the history books (Draculea, in fifteenth-century Romanian). Did you read Mr. Stoker's book? I'm thinking, no; you don't strike me as a reader. But if you are interested, you can check out a couple of the hundreds of movies inspired by your legacy. The one by Universal Studios is hokey, but a classic: *Was he beast . . . man . . . or vampire?*

You might prefer the 1970 remake, *Love at First Bite*, because the actor who plays you, George Hamilton, is tan and good looking. Or at least he was good looking when he made that movie, before all the sun damage. (Please don't kill me if George Hamilton is no longer good looking.)

I wonder what goes through your mind, when you wake up in the morning, look out your castle window onto a sunny, autumnal day, and see all those rotting corpses? Is it hard to keep your breakfast down? Does the sight of your depravity give you pause? And if not, does that mean that your other feelings are blunted as well? What happens, for example, when you see an adorable kitten? Or two old people holding hands? Has anyone ever dared to ask, "How do you feel?" Really, Mr. Impaler, has it ever occurred to you to seek therapy?

Another reason for my writing—though I hesitate to bring this up given what you did to your second cousin Vladivostok II—is that I think, well, I think we may be related. Hear me out and then tell me, please, that I am wrong. When I was a little girl growing up in Lancaster, Pennsylvania, I fantasized that I didn't belong to the parents who were raising me—an engineer and schoolteacher (*boring*)—but rather I came from royalty. You could argue that most children entertain this fantasy at some point, but then a few years ago one of my sisters traced our family ancestry, and it turns out our father's people hailed from Romania, not far from the principality where you served as prince. Could this mean there is at least a half-truth to my childhood imaginings—that I am, in fact, a descendant of royalty, specifically the ruling family of Vlad Tepes, aka Vlad Dracul. I wish I could shake this thought.

I'll admit, the idea of me having any kind of inherited bloodthirst seems far-fetched; just the sight of the carver at the prime rib station at the buffet gives me the squeamies. Still. Yesterday, I was standing in my kitchen, sipping my first cup of toasted almond coffee, when I noticed a swarm of ants by the cat's bowl. I grabbed the Windex and swiped them all into oblivion. Which begs the question, What is weirder, that in the immediate aftermath I imagined the dead ants' families—their growing concern as they waited for their loved ones to return . . . or that I quickly forgot all about the ants and sat at our kitchen breakfast bar to work a crossword puzzle?

I wonder as I write this letter to you: Are some people born impalers? Or is this propensity a combination of nature and nurture, or the confluence of random particulars? You, for example, are a middle child, and while I don't buy into a lot of pseudo-psychological excuses to justify bad behavior, I do believe there is such a thing as the "Middle Child Syndrome." Stuck between the golden oldest and the spoiled baby of the family, it is easy to understand why you might feel ignored and resentful and willing to go to any extremes to prove yourself a winner. I suspect this is partly why my own middle sister spends every holiday season making hundreds of chocolate peanut butter balls, even after there's no room left in her freezer. (Please don't kill me for comparing you to my odd middle sister.)

Of course, all of us are victims of our parents' mistakes. (*If it's not one thing, it's your mother. Ha!*) In your case, however, it doesn't take a radio psychologist to put the blame squarely and fairly on your dad—Vlad II, prince of Wallachia! It was shocking to read how you, as a teenager, and your kid brother, Radu, were forced to live with Sultan Murad II as political hostages, to make sure your father didn't turn traitor while he was off fighting the Hungarians. By most accounts, the sultan treated you okay, providing you with an education in science, philosophy, and swordsmanship. I must say, your little brother adapted well, making friends with the sultan's son, Mehmet II, and eventually converting to Islam (so typical of the youngest, able to make friends so easily). But in 1448, when you replaced your father as ruler of Wallachia, you couldn't wait to stick it to those Ottomans, clearly an expression you took literally.

Massacred: tens of thousands of Turks and Bulgarians! Even by today's standards, that is an impressive genocide. Some historians argue that you were not exceptionally cruel, but rather doing what you had to do to fight a military force much larger than your own. And then there are some other historians who question the legitimacy of your reported exploits. (Books detailing your cruel acts were among the first bestsellers in the German-speaking territories, but we all know how authors are inclined to embellish for the sake of sales.) Regardless, there are plenty of documented images of those skewered corpses surrounding your castle, and this in the days before Photoshop.

The possibility of fake news aside, no one can doubt your mastery at inspiring both fear and an unfathomable loyalty. Even more puzzling to me than your startling behavior is that of your followers and bedfellows who show you such blind deference and a willingness to enforce your horrible agendas. When you demand of them on a whim, "Impale that fellow over there, the bedraggled one with red hair who looks a bit queer," and they say, "Yes, Vlad. No problem, Vlad," do you ever look at them and think, *Well, I know I'm crazy evil, but what happened to your souls? When did all of you make your own deals with the devil?*

But maybe I have it all wrong. Maybe you truly see yourself as a good guy. I recently read about a study in which neuroscientists used brain imaging to test for empathy. The scientists asked participants to rank the degree in which they experienced certain emotions, including their ability to understand and share the feelings of others. Then the participants were given an EEG test while being shown images of neutral and pained faces (though they were instructed to focus on something other than the faces, to distract from the test's real purpose). While the rich and powerful participants reported themselves to be more empathetic, their brain scans actually revealed diminished neural responses to others' pain. As one of the neuroscientists explained, "These findings suggest that empathy, at least some early component of it, is reduced among those who are higher in status."

This discrepancy could explain one mystery: how people in positions of authority, despite the lessons of history, continue to do horrible things—turn away others in need, abuse women, cultivate war, facilitate the destruction of the planet, and even go out of their way to make sure certain people can't pee in peace in a public restroom—and still manage not to hate themselves with the white hot intensity of a thousand television cameras.

I have to admit, I wouldn't mind having tons of money and power, but it scares me—the possibility of becoming one of those people who thinks they have more empathy than everyone else, when clearly their brain scans prove otherwise. And call me a softie, but I really like the feeling I get when I see an adorable kitten or old people holding hands. Is it possible, my potential Romanian ancestor, that you used to feel the same? Did you start out a decent human being, then whoosh down some slippery slope of black ice? As someone who quite possibly shares your bloodline, I worry—How many whittled posts away am I, are any of us, from turning into someone like you?

Nature, nurture, the geography and circumstances of our birth, the Ottomans. I imagine people could spend a lifetime reflecting on the origins and causes of cruelty, and never find a satisfying answer. I am sure this letter is already trying your limited patience, but it has evoked one last thought that I would like to communicate. Maybe, just maybe, the vanquished and impaled are not alone in their profound pain and misery.

Mr. Impaler, when you are home in your castle in the afterlife, the air thick with the stench of victory, do you sometimes wish you could breathe more freely? Can you imagine a time when your legacy gives way to a brighter future? As you dip your bread in the blood of others, does it ever cross your mind, the possibility of rekindling your humanity—the hope, however faint, of finding redemption sometime in the scope of eternity?

Sincerely,
Joni B. Cole

PS. From the historical images I've seen of you, I think you and my great aunt on my father's side bear a striking resemblance, but please don't kill me for saying that.

Winning Women

I had so wanted to look nice.

Flash backward about twenty years. I was flying to St. Louis to give two talks—one to a business organization called Winning Women and one to the Junior Girl Scouts of southeastern Missouri. The irony of being invited to address women executives and ten-year-old girls who earned badges for community service was not lost on me. I have never been able to hold a job for more than two years, and my last civic duty was glaring at a smoker outside Applebee's. But I had recently created a three-volume book series that exposed the realities of a day in the life of thousands of women from across the country and from all walks of life, and this accomplishment obscured my own reality, which was that I spent a good part of my days self-soothing by staring into the open fridge, plus I was terrified of public speaking.

To make up for my lack of suitability as a motivational speaker, not to mention months of neglecting my personal appearance, I was committed to making an effort.

Most of my effort started twenty-four hours before my flight. I decided to color my fading, yellow hair, partly because it seemed ungracious to fly my graying roots halfway across the country on someone else's tab, and partly because I wanted to look fifteen years younger.

Usually when I dye my hair, I choose the medium blonde shade by Natural Match. But wasn't "medium" just another way of saying "average," a shade for women who not only didn't win much, but didn't even like competition and choked at the first sign of it? Yes, that was me, but I didn't need to advertise it. So I decided to go with a "warmer" blonde tone, thinking I would coordinate my hair color with the arrival of summer. Maybe it would even create the illusion of a sunny disposition.

At first I was hoping it was just bad lighting. But when I looked at my newly dyed hair in the bathroom mirror, and then in every other mirror in the house, and on the visor of my Prius, it was still there—a distinctly brassy hue.

This was not the kind of brass associated with top military personnel or expensive floor lamps. This was the kind of brass that brought to mind a boy I'll call Joey Delong, and his dented trumpet. Joey was last chair of the brass section in my middle school band. Because I was the worst flute player in the band, my own chair sat adjacent to Joey's, our spit-filled embouchures creating a discord of windy toots, blasts, and wrong notes. Plus, Joey was a hoodlum. Once, at an away game, he got drunk and threw up in my open flute case.

I retrieved the discarded box of hair dye from the bathroom trash. There was my mistake, explained on an overlooked three-dollars-off coupon good toward my next purchase of Natural Match. "Choose a warmer formula to add RED tones . . ." read the copy on the coupon. Oh no, I realized, a second grader could have predicted this disastrous outcome. My preexisting hair color was yellow. The "warmer" dye added red tones. Yellow plus red equals orange.

The next part of my effort had to do with my legs. Five long winter months of no exposure to the sun, blast-furnace heat, and being too lazy to moisturize had left my skin the color and texture of moon rock. If I was to expose my calves beneath a skirt without the inconvenience of nylons, I would need a tan. Specifically, a fake tan, which I had purchased in an aerosol can at CVS earlier that day, at the same time I picked up the hair dye.

Learning from past mistakes, this time I made a point to read the instructions, including the copy on the inserts. "Spray the tanning lotion on your palm then quickly and evenly apply it to your skin to avoid streaking." I aimed the can's pinhole toward my palm. A mound of poo-colored foam peaked in my hand. No time to reconsider, I started rubbing it into my legs.

But no matter which way I rubbed—in sweeping up-and-down strokes and then frantic, concentric circles—the fake tan wouldn't apply evenly. Parts of my legs remained light, while other parts were smeared dark brown, like the walls next to the crib of some deranged, diaperless baby. The more foam I applied, the darker the streaks. In desperation, I skipped the first step of spraying the foam into my palm and aimed it directly at the remaining patches of moon rock.

A few minutes later I emerged from the bathroom. This was not the look I had hoped for—middle-school-band atop feces. Perhaps, I thought ruefully, I should have started my effort sooner. Perhaps this effort should have included an appointment with a hair care *professional*, and a visit to one of those spray-tan places where you're misted with a bronze glow, then patted down by an attendant.

I had read an article about how movie stars get spray-on tans before they appear at award shows. At the time, I wondered about the safety of spraying chemical dyes directly into your pores. A mental picture formed of Charlize Theron and Nicole Kidman on the Red Carpet, waving to their fans, only instead of arms they had flippers. Things could always be worse, I told myself, trying to maintain some perspective. At least I didn't have spray-tan appendages.

At the airport, my confidence plummeted even further. The infrequent times I fly, I usually travel in jeans, but today I wore a loose black skirt and a stretchy white wrap shirt. A simple, stylish outfit, I thought that morning when I extracted it from my closet, an outfit for the contemporary winning woman on the go.

Who was I kidding? I thought now, waiting at the boarding gate and eating a cruller. These were my pig-out clothes. The past year of deadlines, doughnuts, and delusional thinking that I could still eat anything I wanted without consequences, had taken its toll on my middle. My skirt had an elastic waistband. My shirt's front pleats were designed to camouflage two stomach rolls that rippled over the waistband of my Spanx Thigh-Shaper panties like a capital B.

I caught myself scowling at the petite Japanese businesswoman in line in front of me. She wore a tailored navy suit and a Bluetooth earpiece peeking out from her sleek, black hair. Even her carry-on luggage was trim, a fashionable powder-blue case on wheels. You hardly ever see fat Japanese women, I thought, adjusting my own lumpy shoulder bag like a pack saddle on a donkey. They always seem slim and half my size, and probably don't even have a word for Spanx. It occurred to me, if I ever traveled to Japan, I would be the fattest woman in the entire country, a country of 127 million people.

On the plane, things went from bad to worse. I spent most of the flight going over my Winning Women speech, which I had spent weeks writing and rewriting, and practicing in front of my reluctant family. Because of my fear of public speaking, I had overcompensated by scripting every word and stage direction—"Hello." (*Smile!*) "It's a pleasure to be here." (*Stand up straight and have fun!*)

At some earlier point in time, I remembered liking my speech, but now it seemed silly and trite, like I was some middle-aged Up with People wannabe, only tone deaf and with fewer ideals. I could just see it now: a roomful of three hundred Winning Women, all pretending to listen to me, but secretly multitasking. Five minutes into my fifty-minute talk, the organization's president would usher me away from the podium.

"So sorry," she'd say, pausing to check her schedule on her BlackBerry, "but our organization is committed to work-life balance, and I'm afraid you don't qualify as quality time."

I put my speech away, intending to relax, but then I splattered coffee down the front of my white shirt. In the lavatory, I saturated a bunch of Wet Naps in the undrinkable water and managed to soak out the stains, but we were landing in less than an hour. The stretchy fabric over my breasts was covered with big, wet blotches. Whoever was meeting me at the airport would think I was lactating, like one of those women you read about in the tabloids who figure out how to get pregnant even after they qualify for social security benefits. "Determined great-grandma delivers sextuplets!"

When I returned to my seat, no one seemed to notice that I was wearing what amounted to a skin-tight, see-through shirt. At first I was relieved, but then it occurred to me—why hadn't anyone noticed, not even the young guy in the seat beside me? He was watching an action-adventure movie on the flight, the kind of Hollywood blockbuster that specializes in gratuitous violence and objectifying women. Yet here I was, only an armrest away, my cold nipples protruding so far they were practically sitting in first class, and it was like I was invisible. No, I didn't want people staring at my breasts. But I did want breasts that people would want to stare at, if that sort of thing wasn't frowned upon.

Now wouldn't that be a fine message for the Junior Girl Scouts, I thought. One of the Winning Women (who was also a Girl Scout leader) had asked me to serve as one of their role model speakers at their regional meeting. The girls were earning their Career Badges, so I was to talk about my job and offer inspiration.

"You can be anything you want to be!" I would tell the Junior Girl Scouts. "But what difference does it make if you can't even get noticed in a see-through shirt?"

By the time the plane arrived in St. Louis, any fortitude I had brought along on this journey had abandoned me somewhere over the Midwest. I started humping my carry-on sack toward baggage claim, all the other arriving and departing passengers only serving to remind me of my own insignificance. The petite Asian woman with the powder-blue case was long gone. No baggage claim for her, given her entire tiny corporate wardrobe could fit on the head of a pin.

Near the luggage carousel, I spotted one of the Winning Women holding up a sign with my name on it. She looked to be in her early thirties, and probably had two-point-five children and ran a Fortune 100 company. No doubt she also was super nice, which only made things worse. She glanced around the crowded carousel, but didn't see me, or more likely didn't recognize me from the picture on my website. And why should she? I thought. At the time the photo was taken, I didn't look like a spray-tanned Joey Delong.

Standing there, I wished with all my heart that I had never agreed to be a guest speaker for Winning Women. I wished that I hadn't promised to be a role model for the Junior Girl Scouts of southeastern Missouri. But it was too late for that kind of thinking. I had committed to making an effort. It was time to earn my own badge of courage.

Flash forward about twenty years, through all the subsequent times I have been asked to give talks, or found myself behind a podium, wondering what in the hell I was doing there. I always take heart in what I did in that moment two decades earlier.

I walked over to the polished young executive holding the Winning Women sign with my name on it, and I just followed my script and stage directions.

"Hello." (Smile!) "It's a pleasure to be here." (Stand up straight and have fun!)

〜

Let It Lie

"There's someone in the ladies' room using nunchucks." My daughter Esme tells me when she rejoins me at our table in an oversized café where we are meeting for Americanos and pastries.

"Nunchucks?" I repeat, not sure I had heard her correctly.

"Yes, nunchucks. This lady is practicing a bunch of moves by the sinks. I had to go around her to wash my hands."

If I recall correctly, nunchucks are a ninja weapon, made up of two hard rods, each about a foot long and connected by a short chain. Martial artist Bruce Lee helped them gain popularity through his kung fu movies. So did one of the Teenage Mutant Ninja Turtles, stars of television and film and a live musical tour in the nineties. The appeal of these sewer-dwelling superheroes was lost on me, but I do remember reading in the entertainment news that Michelangelo, the mutant turtle known for wielding nunchucks, had to switch weapons when the group toured parts of Europe. Apparently, in saner countries, nunchucks have been banned in public places, along with other lethal weapons.

I ask Esme, "Did this woman in the bathroom seem . . . scary?" In my mind's eye I can already see the story on CNN's Breaking News:

Nunchucks Attack in Small-Town Café!
"I never thought it could happen here," said one distraught patron who was with her daughter when the attack occurred. "I barely escaped with an ugly bruise."

"She didn't look all that scary to me," Esme interrupts my mental catastrophizing. "Actually, it looked pretty cool."

I glance around the café. Everything looks business-as-usual, though this is not your typical Vermont coffee shop, or rather it is, but on anabolic steroids. The place offers that same wholesome, recycled-napkins vibe you see in all the places advertised in pamphlets in Vermont-run rest stops along the interstate. But this café is comparable to a full-sized restaurant, plus it is connected to a world-renowned baking store. In summers, the café and store are packed, as evidenced on this Sunday morning in June. Here we all are, a swarm of locals and tourists, just trying to enjoy eight-dollar lattes and buy unbleached flour in peace.

"Maybe she's going to do a martial arts demonstration," I say, groping for a rational explanation. On a regular basis, the baking store offers bread-making classes and cookie-decorating contests, so a demonstration was not out of the question. But a nunchaku demo? Was this a new way to knead dough?

I am trepidatious but feel compelled to check out the nunchucks lady for myself.

My first impression: Patty Hearst, but before Patty Hearst was brainwashed by a terrorist organization. She has the famous kidnapped victim's same broad face and wavy brown hair, but the eyes do not look all that defiant or crazy. Also, she is wearing a homespun denim jumper with lilac Crocs, a fashion statement more Vermont than guerrilla attire. Most notably, she is, indeed, wielding lethal-looking nunchucks.

"Excuse me," I murmur. The restroom's limited size requires that I have to scooch around her to reach the small bank of stalls. Patty Hearst twitches me a smile, not missing a beat as she whips the rods around her waist and in figure eights. *Excuse me.* Why am I the one making excuses, like some late arrival to the opera?

I close myself in the accessible bathroom, a roomier place to collect my thoughts. Should I say something to this woman? *This is not acceptable behavior in a public restroom!* Or maybe I could be more politic? *Perhaps you might want to practice your nunchucks elsewhere, say a dojo or the middle of a pasture.* I could report her to an authority figure, but who would that be? The ponytailed barista who served us our Americanos? Or one of the hard-working bread-makers on display behind the bakery's glass wall? *Tap, tap, tap. Could you come out here for a moment? And please bring your rolling pin, just in case.*

I wait a respectable amount of time in the stall, then flush the toilet that I did not use. I would not want Patty Hearst to think I just came into the bathroom to spy on her. At the hand dryer, I brace for a blow. This is just wrong, I think, not about someone practicing nunchucks in a ladies' room but that a busy bakery like this famous tourist spot would have such an inadequately sized ladies' room. The five stalls and two sinks can barely accommodate the locals, let alone the swell of tourists, plus the occasional ninja.

The nunchucks situation reminds me of another experience that included equally odd bathroom behavior. That story, however, is set in the Dreamland building, where I rent a room on the second floor for my writer's center. Here I teach my in-person classes, or just hang out, rearranging the magnetic poetry on the mini-fridge. The other upstairs offices in Dreamland are rented mostly by healers: a reflexologist, two massage therapists, plus a loud-talking mental health counselor whose voice permeates the thin walls (so much for patient confidentiality). The other end of the second floor is taken up by a capacious yoga studio whose students must come to our side of the building when they need to use the single-occupant, second-floor bathroom.

"Did you see someone left a wad of used toilet paper on the floor of the bathroom?" The question came from the reflexologist, who intercepted me in the hall as I was arriving to teach a morning workshop. We were standing near the threshold of her office, which, despite being the closest to the bathroom, always smells pleasantly of essential oils.

"Well, it wasn't me," I responded defensively. The reflexologist is a lovely and spiritual person. The tone with which she asked me her question was as non-accusatory as I imagine her response to some of her client's disgusting feet. Still, when someone broaches such a subject, you cannot help but feel guilty.

"You know, this isn't the first time I've seen this happen," she added. "Whoever it is, their pitta is definitely out of balance."

Naturally, our exchange prompted me to see this affront for myself. And there it was, a small, dampish clump, resting at the foot of the toilet. To get a better visual, picture a dropped tissue an ex-wife might have been clenching during her former husband's funeral. Yes, the woman had shed a few tears for the sake of their children, but her ex was a cheater who had gone on to marry his personal trainer.

Once the reflexologist brought the wads to my attention, it became impossible to unsee them. Whereas before I might have overlooked them or assumed they were just a bit of dampish detritus, not so anymore. Indeed, every time I went to the restroom I was on high alert. And the mystery wadder did not disappoint. The crumples continued to appear, not every day but with enough consistency that even I—who was not in the building nearly as often as the other Dreamlanders—recognized that this, clearly, was a thing; a thing that had escalated into a second-floor scandal.

"It's disgusting!" This time when the reflexologist intercepted me in the hall, her tone was far less charitable. She snapped on a pair of disposable gloves, readying to remove the latest offense from the bathroom floor. This was but one more difference between me and my healer neighbors. At this point, I was equally disturbed—even consumed by the situation at work—yet there was no way I was going to take matters into my own hands, at least not in such a literal way.

"Who do you think it is?" the reflexologist asked me for the umpteenth time.

"Some nut job who should be banned from the building." This response came not from me, but from one of the massage therapists who was walking by us toward his office, carrying a basket of freshly laundered towels.

"Well it's not me!" I felt compelled to yell after him.

The challenge was that dozens of people used the upstairs restroom, and none of us who rented space had time to stand sentinel. Of course, the tenants on our side of the second floor had our suspicions, most of them directed at the yoga people. We had no real evidence to support these feelings, other than the fact they were foreigners, immigrants from another part of Dreamland. On one hand, we understood their plight—their end of the hall had no toilet. On the other hand, the yoga people caused lines to form in front of the bathroom before and after every class, and we needed to look out for our own.

One day, I arrived at work and discovered a sign taped to the bathroom mirror, smack in the middle of the glass.

PLEASE PUT ALL USED TOILET PAPER IN THE TOILET. THANK YOU.

Later, I learned that this was the reflexologist's doing, which did not surprise me. The "please" and "thank you" fit with her style. I appreciated her taking the initiative but had my reservations. Would this sign do more harm than good? If I were a visitor to Dreamland, say a writing student or a client in need of a massage, wouldn't such a sign beg the question: What kind of professionals have clientele who need to be told such things?

Regardless, more weeks passed, and the sign did nothing to deter our wadder. She must have known the message was intended for her. It was not like those other signs ("Employees must wash hands") that could be directed at any number of offenders. How did it make her feel, I wondered, to have to confront her aberrant behavior every time she tried to look around it to see herself in the mirror?

Then one morning I caught her! I caught the wadder, and there was no room for doubt. I had just finished washing a mug in the bathroom sink, taking note of the clean floor. Less than a minute later I returned to the bathroom to fill the coffee pot, but by then the door was closed, with a yoga mat propped beside it. I waited in the hall until the person emerged. The woman retrieved her mat and scurried past me, head down. And that is when I saw it—a little damp wad at the foot of the toilet! No one else could have had the time to use this bathroom in the interim of my two visits.

"Hey! Hey!" I called out, louder than necessary. We were only a few yards apart, but she kept on walking. "Stop," I said, aware of my pounding heart. The woman hesitated then turned to face me. *Colorless* was the word that popped into my head. The woman seemed lacking all vitality, from her meatless frame, to her pallid complexion, to the faded wisps of curls that passed for her hair.

"Are you talking to me?" she asked.

"You need to put your used toilet paper in the toilet," I told her. If I had thought those words looked ridiculous on a sign taped to the mirror, that was nothing compared to hearing myself speak them aloud. "I know it's you," I soldiered on. "Stop leaving your toilet paper on the floor."

"What an odd thing to say." The woman's flat tone and frozen stance gave nothing—and everything—away.

"Just, just stop doing it," I said, faltering. This was not how I had imagined my confrontation with the wadder. I would be cool as tempered steel. My fellow tenants would hail me as the hero of Dreamland. And with the situation resolved, I would encourage my office neighbors to open their hearts to the yoga people. "Let us no longer foster division," I would tell them, "as long as they keep to their end of the second floor."

As it turned out, the healers and I had been right about the culprit being one of the yoga people. But everything else felt wrong. "That person's not right in the head." When I was growing up, this was what my mom used to say whenever we encountered someone who clearly suffered from some form of mental disorder. Her words came to mind as I confronted the wadder. It had to be humiliating to be accosted like this, yet she simply stared at me for a few moments, then turned and headed once more toward the yoga studio. *She's not right in the head.* It was a painful sight to watch her walk away, her body as thin as a winter twig, and probably just as snappable.

In the bakery, my daughter and I continue to people watch as we linger over our Americanos. Women enter and emerge from the ladies' room, all of them seemingly unscathed by Patty Hearst and her nunchucks. *Move along. Nothing to see here.* Maybe they simply do not want to get involved, but I hope their inaction has more to do with tolerance and acceptance. You just never know why someone feels the need to practice nunchucks in a public bathroom—or, for that matter, drop their used toilet paper on the floor—so there is always the worry that calling them out could do more psychological harm than good.

In the aftermath of my own confrontation with the wadder, the crumples stopped appearing on the floor of the second-floor bathroom. I watched for the pale, wispy-curled woman in the hall, but she, like her small, soiled droppings, seemed to be gone. This was good news for my office neighbors, but I could not stop fretting. I even created a psychological profile for the wadder, something I felt qualified to do having binge-watched twelve seasons of *Criminal Minds*. Given that the woman was a dabber rather than a wiper, I deduced that she had intimacy issues.

Her behavior also was consistent with someone who suffers from severe OCD and feels the need to control every aspect of her life.

In FBI lingo, the wadder fit into the category of an "organized" criminal, that is someone who is antisocial but knows right from wrong; someone who is not insane but shows no remorse. As is often the case on *Criminal Minds*, when subjects are provoked they feel the need to escalate their crimes. This raised the question—If the wadder ever did return to Dreamland, what might she leave next on the floor? Nothing, I was sure, that I cared to step in.

More worrisome—much more worrisome—was a question that haunted me for weeks. What if the wadder never returned to Dreamland? What if I had driven her from yoga class, an activity that must have offered her some sense of well-being? What if I had deprived her of a behavior essential to her need for control? I thought of my own compulsion to knock on wood whenever I tempted fate; how I counted in my head to alleviate anxiety; how I always need to touch certain markers on my running route. What would I do if someone called me out for doing these things that, however seemingly illogical, help me to keep it together? I chided myself for my insensitivity and my big mouth. What was the big deal anyway, having to step around a few soiled, little wads?

At the bakery, Patty Hearst emerges from the bathroom, accompanied by a store manager with a name tag and flour-dusted apron to prove it. The manager must have asked her to leave because she heads toward the exit, her nunchucks dangling in defeat by her side.

"People are strange," my daughter comments as we bus our table.

"True," I answer, remembering the enormous relief I felt that morning after I entered Dreamland's second-floor bathroom and discovered the reappearance of a small, damp crumple by the foot of the toilet. The wadder had returned! I had not driven her to the desperate act I had feared the most. Since then, she and I have crossed paths a few times in the hall, but neither of us acknowledges the other. I am more than happy to let things lie.

Outside by my car, I watch Patty Hearst cross the parking lot in her denim jumper and lilac Crocs. I wish she would do some more of her fancy ninja moves, especially now that she has a healthy amount of space. Instead, she tosses her nunchucks into a car that looks like it's on its last legs and drives off. Who knows if she will ever return to this bustling bakery, given how the manager had clearly told her to leave. I can only imagine how a person in such circumstances must feel embarrassed, or chastened, or maybe something worse, but this time, thankfully, not by me.

Party Like It's 2044

I shuffled through the early February snow-slush to my mailbox and the effort did not disappoint. There in the mix was what looked to be an early birthday card in a bright-pink envelope, along with an over-sized flyer from a local car dealer advertising a blowout sale ("Drive away today in a brand-new Subaru!"). Also in the mix was a letter with the return address: the Cremation Society of Vermont.

Back inside, I eagerly opened the pink card. "Dear Joni," wrote one of my good friends, "I know how much you love your birthday, and it's quite refreshing, especially given our advanced years . . ." The image on the card showed one of those wrinkled dogs. Jesus, I thought, if I was hoping for something more upbeat, I probably should have just opened the letter from the Cremation Society. This friend, however, got one thing right. I do love my birthday and always have, minus the one with the red velvet cake incident better left forgotten. But my friend's comment about our advanced age felt like a coffin dropped on my enthusiasm, and right when the arrival of my first card should have marked the kick-off of my annual month-long celebration of my birth.

. . . *advanced years.* I put the card on my windowsill, a nice reminder of my good friend, and that I am nearing death. And by nearing death, as this card handily reminded me, we weren't talking about dying from a sudden illness or accident, but simply dying from old age. Plain old age, meaning if I dropped dead tomorrow, people would read my obituary and, I hope, feel horrible, but no one would be thinking, *What a terrible tragedy. She died so young.*

Any other day, I would have tossed the unsolicited letter from the Cremation Society of Vermont, but its arrival on the launch of my birthday month seemed suspiciously significant, an omen in the form of junk mail.

Knock, knock.

Who's there?

The friendly folks at the Cremation Society, wishing you a happy birthday and also a bit of timely advice—don't bother with Subaru's blowout sale.

I opened the letter, likely one of the first times I willingly stared the inevitability of death—my death—head on. This was a luxury; I was well aware. A number of my friends, several of them younger than me, have circumstances that have pressed this issue upon them, while I have merrily avoided things like deciding what to do with my remains. This has allowed me, emotionally speaking, to stay at the age where I am more focused on buying expensive age-defying creams, which would be a terrible investment if I was to think too hard about how little time I have left to let them work their wonders.

"Dear Informed Consumer . . ." the letter from the Cremation Society began. Back in my days as a copywriter, I used to write these types of marketing letters, so I was aware that even the deferential salutation was part of the soft sell. And the flattery worked! These people assumed I was informed, and this before they had told me a single thing about their services.

It turned out the Cremation Society also understood the trouble I've seen. "The death of a loved one is one of the hardest things a family has to face . . ." No argument there. So to help me prepare for this tragic circumstance, they assured me that they were here to give me peace of mind, whether I used their services on an as-needed basis or chose to become a member of their society. The latter option intrigued me. Other than society at large, I had rarely claimed membership in any type of club or association. But would this be the type of club I would want to join? It seemed it might attract a bit of a peculiar population—what kind of people opt to gather on a regular basis to talk about cremation and ashes, rather than, say, go bowling, or discuss their book club pick? And if I did join the Cremation Society of Vermont, would they send me a free tote or coffee mug like public radio provides its members? I really wouldn't want to be reminded of incinerated bodies every time I went shopping or sipped my coffee. Plus, exactly how many cremations would it take to amortize the cost of membership?

The letter closed by encouraging me to complete the accompanying questionnaire. Thus far, the tone of the letter had been so comforting, so compelling, I found myself seeking a pen almost against my will. *Yes, Cremation Society of Vermont*, I imagined myself nodding in a zombie-like trance, *I wish to be cremated . . . and I wish to pay in advance.*

Question 1: "What is your age?"

Question 2: "What is your annual income?"

Gone, just like that, was the caring overtone of the cover letter, knocked out by this one-two punch of hard numbers.

Question 3: "Have you ever been responsible for making cremation arrangements?"

I had not, which was obviously a blessing, but it also raised the question, why hadn't anyone in my family entrusted me with this issue? My dad had been cremated, but no one had consulted me. Maybe because he was still sending me money to help buy my daughters a few extra Christmas presents, even when I was well into my forties?

Question 4: "Would you ever consider cremation for yourself?"

Sure, I thought, after I'm dead. No doubt the folks at the Cremation Society had heard this lame joke a million times before, but already I had lost my motivation for going down this responsible road. Why should I have to deal with such a heavy issue right at the start of my birthday month? Shouldn't birthdays be all about celebrating?

As February slogged on, the short winter days were brightened, sort of, by the arrival of several more early birthday cards. One of them depicted a birthday cake on fire, given the requisite number of candles. Another depicted a wizened chicken asking itself, "Wait, why did I cross the road?" Most notable among the greetings, my friend Ed had not only sent a card, but he also had gone to the trouble of creating an actuarial table to calculate my remaining life expectancy. As such, Ed had gifted me with the following information: "You will live another 22.5 years and will die on Thursday, September 15th, 2044, at the age of 86.5. Your life is 74 percent over, or put another way, you have 26 percent of your life left."

This was a bummer, not just the thought of my life being 74 percent over, but that I would die in September. Now that month would forever be tainted, and it used to be the start of my favorite season, autumn in New England. Now though, whenever I saw the leaves turn their vibrant reds and yellows and oranges, I would probably think of it not as foliage, but as a degradation of chlorophyll, abscission, and a reminder of my own ultimate downfall.

Enclosed with the card, Ed also had enthusiastically shared the figures he'd computed for his own actuarial table, which showed him living longer than me, given he is a couple years younger. To my birthday greeting he'd added this sweet personal message, "Now, what am I going to do with those last two years and one month when I can't call you up to have lunch?"

"Are Your Affairs in Order?" A few weeks into my birthday month, this posting appeared on my town's online listserv, amid all the usual listings of snowblowers for sale, tutors for hire, requests for house cleaner recommendations, political feuds, yoga classes, more yoga classes, and more yoga classes. Given the birthday cards accumulating on my windowsill, most of them reminding me of my imminent demise, I no longer found it possible to ignore this pressing question. Were my affairs in order? The answer was a definitive no, but then again, what affairs did I have to organize?

One click on the listing brought me to the website of a small local company offering a free, thirty-minute webinar about creating a will. I studied the photo of the company's founder, a lawyer named Alicia. She reminded me of my more practical, put-together friends who never let their gas tanks go below half-empty, who can pull off a pussy bow, and who always decline a second glass of wine, all of which makes me irrationally resistant to their sound advice. But that was before, when time was on my side and my birthday cake was not a fire hazard.

"Sixty-eight percent of Americans do not have a will." It was the Monday before my birthday and I was sitting at my kitchen counter, making myself watch Alicia's free, thirty-minute webinar. Her opening statistic was a grabber, for sure, but then I thought: Wait a second. Does that 68 percent include babies?

As the webinar continued, Alicia talked me and the other online listeners through the basics of why having a will is so important and what is needed to create one. She was well spoken and convincing, but the language of will-making kept stealing my focus. Why was it that after you die, your children turn into "beneficiaries" and gifts become "bequests"? How curious, that "intestate" and "intestine" shared the same root word. And then I got to thinking about the term "notary public." Why tag on the word "public" when the word notary already said it all?

Toward the end of the webinar, Alicia touted her company's featured service, a proprietary online program that allows clients to create their own will, without the need for a lawyer. This program is ideal for people who do not have a lot of assets, who do not co-own properties or goods, and who will not be creating a trust. Basically, Alicia was offering a DIY will that was perfect for people like me. And the cost, just forty dollars!

Should I? Shouldn't I? The price seemed remarkably low, but I wasn't a DIY type of person. I didn't even trust myself to change my printer cartridge, so what business did I have creating my own legal document?

"As a thank you for participating in this webinar," Alicia added, "you'll receive a 20 percent discount when you use this program to write your own will."

A 20 percent discount? It was almost as if Alicia was giving away wills!

I clicked on the link for making my own will and was off to a good start getting my affairs in order until I reached Question 5: "Would you like to designate any special bequests to a person or entity?" The question flummoxed me because I am someone who doesn't own a lot of stuff. I am a minimalist who prefers an inordinate amount of blank space on her walls and in the rooms of her condo. I am not even a big fan of furniture.

"For Chrissakes, get a coffee table!" This was the refrain of my old buddy Mike, whenever he attended parties at my house. "Where the hell am I supposed to put my drink?" Mike died a few years ago, but I still smile at the memory of how, at some point in almost every gathering, he ended up spilling his Old Fashioned, dropping his pants, or starting a feud that would be forgotten, or at least forgiven, by morning. In retrospect, it occurred to me that maybe my lack of a coffee table deserved some of the blame for his inebriated behavior.

To answer Question 5, I did a mental inventory of my belongings, none of which seemed to rise to the connotation of a bequest. That was not to say that I didn't possess treasures, which I did, all of them appraised highly in sentimental value. In fact, even as I was making my DIY will, one of my favorite possessions was staring at me from across the room, where it rested on the back of the couch. This treasure was an oversized stuffed animal, a plush pig that once belonged to my mom and made me think of her every day. But was it really necessary to designate which one of my two grown daughters inherited it?

"Mother told me she wanted me to have the plush pig," I imagined my firstborn declaring to her sister, as she squished the stuffed animal to her chest.

"Liar!" My younger daughter grabs at the plushie. "I'm sure Mother meant it for me."

"You'll be hearing from my lawyer!"

"I'll see you in court!"

I closed my computer, feeling deflated and without assigning a single bequest. Creating a DIY will was yet another responsibility that would have to wait for another day. As much as I appreciated Alicia's good sense and her discounted pricing, I didn't want her intruding on my birthday month any more than I wanted to buddy up to the people at the Cremation Society of Vermont who had tried to flatter me into letting them turn me into ash. In the kitchen where I was sitting, I happened to glance down at the floor, which was strewn with toast crumbs and cat hair. A thought occurred: What if I keeled over right now? Then whoever finds me would know what a slob of a housekeeper I was, but they wouldn't have a clue what to do with my corpse.

My big day arrived—February 24th!—as had more birthday greetings by snail mail and online. I made room on the sill for the newest card, this one depicting a parking meter. It read: "You may be aging, but at least you're not expired." What was I missing? I thought. A sense of humor, obviously, but what annoyed me when I looked at this assortment of cards was the irony of the situation, meaning that after someone dies, we all talk a good game about their funeral being a celebration of their life, yet in most of the years leading up to that inevitability, we behave like a birthday is a cause for mourning. I recalled a scene from a previous February years ago, when I had been painting a bedroom in the house my husband and I had recently bought. I was feeling joyful, rolling on soft yellow paint in this upstairs room full of possibilities. Maybe soon it would belong to a baby yet to be conceived, or allow our parents and other overnight guests a place to sleep that didn't involve an air mattress on the living room floor.

A friend whose birthday was a few days after mine stopped by, allegedly to help paint and keep me company. "How are you going to celebrate your big day?" I had asked her.

"We're getting so old," she cried, throwing herself on the bed. We? I thought. Why did she have to sweep me along in her flood of tears? More to the point, that was the year we both turned thirty-two.

I made myself a margarita—a little pre-celebration to shake off my mood and gear up for the party I had planned for myself that evening at a Mexican restaurant. Birthday resolution number one, I thought, stay away from people who bring me down. This might be a challenge, given the row of depressing cards on my windowsill, all from people I love. As I sipped my drink and donned my party dress, my imagination got the best of me. I envisioned the restaurant where my friends and I would be gathering, only it wasn't furnished with real tables adorned with flowers and noisemakers, but actuarial tables covered in spreadsheets.

"Welcome, señora," the Grim Reaper greeted me with a grin full of decayed teeth. A seating chart rested on his host stand. It was marked with little black crosses that assigned a seat to me and each of my party guests, determined by a calculus of their age, gender, family history, and health habits. "Please follow me," the Reaper pulled out a chair at table

2044, my place of honor indicated with a party hat bedazzled with black rhinestones that spelled out: "HAPPY DEATHDAY!"

"Señora is much loved, is she not?" He swept his skeletal arm at the surrounding actuarial tables, occupied by my friends and family. I refused to follow his gaze. I didn't want to know who was seated where— whose seat was nearest the exit.

An hour or so later, my cell phone rang as Helmut and I were driving to the party.

"Happy birthday, Mom! I love you."

I let my daughter know that I was having a good birthday because I knew she wanted to hear this, and because I should be having a good day, considering the fact that another birthday was a whole lot better than the alternative.

"Just so you know," I told my daughter, "when I die I want to be cremated." There, now I could croak with at least one of my affairs in order.

"Don't say that," my daughter insisted. "You're never going to die."

"Of course not, honey," I reassured her, touched by the conviction in her voice. "I'm never going to die." Finally! Here was the kind of greeting appropriate for one's birthday.

When we reached the restaurant parking lot, I checked my face in the visor mirror and applied fresh lipstick. In my conversation with my daughter, it had felt good to make my end-of-life wishes known, so my plan was to do so again, only this time I would communicate my birthday wishes. Tonight, I vowed, my friends and I were going to celebrate my life, without me having to die first. We were going to eat and drink and get loud. There would be zero talk of decrepitude or demise—mine or anybody else's. Everyone, and I mean everyone, was going to dance on the tables, even if it killed us, and I was going to party like it was 2044.

━⌇━

But Enough about Me

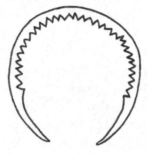

As bad luck would have it, the hostess of this luncheon for women in the arts had seated me next to an elegant woman with silvery blonde hair smoothed back with a tortoiseshell headband. Worn on young girls, the tortoiseshell headband might simply suggest an over-controlling mother who wants her daughter to be perfect in every way. But on women of a certain age, this accessory delivers a clear message: I am a woman of considerable means. Do not presume we are equals. If we did not live in America, where any acknowledgment of class or aristocracy is frowned upon, we would neither move in the same circles, nor occupy this same table as we are now.

I tucked my purse and gym bag under my chair. A quick glance around the private dining room revealed other harbingers of my being outclassed—pearl chokers, linen dresses, pocketbooks with clasps. But unlike the tortoiseshell headband, those items didn't come with parallel rows of sharp little teeth.

"Hello, I'm Marion." Lady Headband paused her conversation with the woman to her right. She extended a creamy hand with prominent blue veins.

"And I'm Amanda." The woman beside her—her silver hair coiffed like a Roman helmet—offered a polite smile. Replace the smile with a contemptuous look, and Amanda reminded me of the formidable lady who had put me in my place when I was at the library last week. My flip-flops had been propped on a low table while I typed on my laptop. "That's a beautiful piece of furniture," the woman had peered down at my feet over her rims. "Very expensive."

This could be the same woman who had looked down on my flip-flops, I thought, but then again I could just be paranoid.

Ours was a round table for eight; its circumference too big to reach across the expanse of white linen and shake hands with everybody. I was the last to arrive, save for the person assigned the seat to my left. The place card for the missing guest read "Beverly," also the name of my former mother-in-law, but given her predilection for clipping coupons, and the fact that she was deceased, I doubted this was her.

It appeared, despite the fact I was menopausal, that I was the youngster in our group. The woman directly across from me looked to be in her two hundreds, her pallor reanimated with a shaky hand—scribbled brows, smeared coral lip lines, two uneven spots of rouge. I wished I was sitting next to her, which would make me look about twenty-two by comparison.

The server appeared, offering a choice of drinks. By the time I'd decided on a cranberry spritzer, the other ladies at my table had resumed their conversations. Eavesdropping, I learned Lady Headband and Amanda had both recently traveled to Japan. Apparently, the Pure Water Temple of Kyoto was beautiful, and worth fighting the crowds.

I looked around the dining room, estimating about one hundred women in attendance. I had assumed I would know a few people here, given that many of my friends are writers or artists of some kind. Like me, they aren't the type to turn down a free lunch, or better yet a free *luncheon*, which implies fare of a higher social status. The only person I recognized, however, was our hostess who wasn't even my friend—she was my landlady. I rented a small space from her to teach writing workshops in one of the many buildings she owns.

Suddenly, I caught on. These people were not women in the arts, not like me anyway, spending the morning at the computer, eking out a few paragraphs of prose, grabbing a shower at the last minute, trying to find something presentable to wear, realizing, too late, that the ruffle on this silk blouse looked like a baby's bib, yanking on some strappy sandals, wondering what would it hurt to put a little wine in a travel mug for the twenty-minute ride to the restaurant, deciding against it, and promising myself (again) that I would go to my exercise class right after this luncheon because I had already paid for the class, and I knew I would never do push-ups and sit-ups on my own because I was a lazy slob and a bad writer and in serious need of some endorphins.

These women, I realized, were patrons of the arts. It all made sense now: our philanthropic hostess; the predominance of elderly, well-appointed guests; the location of this restaurant, not in my economically diverse town, but one upscale town over. Most of the women who lived in this community were not only wealthy, but possessed a daunting degree of civic duty and global responsibility. During elections, for example, they didn't just display campaign signs, they retrieved those signs post-election and turned them into book bags for needy children in Honduras.

"Excuse me." The server reached over my shoulder to deliver a basket of hard-crusted rolls. Good, something to occupy my hands. I took a roll, cracking it in half. With tiny, silver tongs, I retrieved two balls of butter from a chilled bowl. By now it was painfully obvious to me that my seatmate to the left, Beverly, was a No Show. This situation happened to me with peculiar frequency, at wedding receptions, dinner parties, and most recently at a humor-writing conference of four-hundred writers. Every assigned table in the hotel's banquet room was filled with the exception of mine, occupied solely by me and a large, ruddy-faced man with a walking aid who, no doubt, would have switched seats if his gout-riddled feet had allowed mobility. Despite the focus of the conference, I failed to see the humor in this situation.

With no Beverly to turn to, this left me overly dependent on Lady Headband, who was still chatting away with her bestie, Amanda. What, I wondered, could be so fascinating about Japan? Actually I knew the answer to that question, not because I had been there, but because I had recently attended a reading by a novelist who wrote about Japanese women employed as tabletops. Apparently, people pay big money to eat sushi off naked bodies. I learned that this is a long-standing Japanese practice called *nyotaimori*, which some people consider degrading to women, while others view it as a healthy sexual fetish. I could have explained all this to Lady Headband and Amanda, if they had bothered to include me in their conversation. I also could have explained this to my other seatmates, except our over-large table didn't facilitate easy conversation.

"Yes, I said *sushi*," I imagined myself raising my voice for the benefit of the centenarian across from me. "The people at the restaurant eat it right off women's naked bodies."

The server returned, bearing a large tray of bowls above her head.

"What kind of soup is this?" I inquired.

"Chilled asparagus with crème fraiche. It's one of our most popular items."

"It certainly is an astonishing shade of green."

"Fresh cracked pepper?" she asked.

"Oh yes." If only she would stay and talk with me the entire luncheon.

"Enjoy." She glided away, a single bowl remaining on her otherwise empty tray—the fucking No Show's.

As always when surrounded by people of refinement, I found myself affecting their mannerisms. Already, I had used the word "oeuvre," which normally doesn't roll off my tongue. Now I made a point to spoon my soup away from me, tilting it sideways into my mouth.

Plop.

A dollop of green foam landed on the ruffle of my silk blouse. I wiped at it with my napkin, smearing it down the light fabric. In general, I am not a clumsy person, with the exception of spilling food down my front when I am trying to look nice. Likely this is rooted in some deep-seated psychological issue: maybe I'm projecting my social anxiety onto my wardrobe or trying to deflect attention to a flaw not part of my actual person. At the moment, however, I preferred to blame good manners, or more specifically, Marion and her tortoiseshell headband, for the stain on my blouse. This never would have happened if she wasn't ignoring me.

"How do you know our hostess?" I asked, fixing her with the gaze of a locked-on missile.

She looked up, her soup spoon midway to her mouth. "Our husbands are law partners," she said. "We're starting a scholarship program for young artists."

Always the young artists, I thought. Why doesn't anyone care about middle-aged artists?

"Oh really," I said, and then I couldn't think of another thing to say or ask about her scholarship program, try as I might. Looking at her face, a smooth mask of pressed powder, all I could think of was how I needed to start saving for a facelift. An awkward silence followed, or at least it felt awkward to me, given my discomfort with even slight lapses in conversation. I sensed I would soon lose Lady Headband, if I didn't do something fast.

"I'm a writer," I announced. This came out the way a four-year-old might say, "I'm a big girl."

"What do you write?" Lady Headband inquired. This was a perfectly reasonable response, no different from when somebody introduces herself as a teacher, which elicits the natural follow-up, "What do you teach?" Or when someone claims to be a prisoner, prompting the obvious, "Are you a murderer?" Still, I usually dread being asked what I write because whatever confidence I am feeling in my career at that moment is almost always dashed when it becomes clear the person has never heard of me or read any of my work.

"Well," I hesitated, then made a quick decision to talk about my first writing project because it made me seem more socially aware than my other efforts. "Several years ago," I started, "I created a book series that invited hundreds of women across the country to record what they were doing and thinking and feeling on a single day."

"What an interesting idea," Lady Headband gracefully sipped from her spoon.

Yes, it was an interesting idea, I thought, but I wasn't entirely convinced of her sincerity. I felt compelled to prove myself to her.

"The women in the project came from all walks of life," I elaborated. "Funeral directors, nuns, refugees, actors, politicians, detectives, mothers, madams, rodeo riders . . ." Like a geyser, my words kept erupting, until I had detailed every trial and triumph over the six years and fifteen hundred participants it took to complete the three volumes in the book series.

This happens sometimes when I'm feeling awkward or insecure, or even when I'm just being my normal self. I start talking and can't seem to stop, even though I can hear myself going on and on. Sometimes before leaving my house, I will ink the words "hush up" in tiny letters on my palm, in the hopes this will remind me to take a breath. Today, unfortunately, my hands were of no use.

I have been in the position Lady Headband finds herself in now, held hostage by the nonstop talker. First, you are transfixed by the torrent of words, the cluelessness, the solipsism of the speaker. Then you begin to attend to small, previously overlooked details: the number of times she blinks per minute, the pull of her earrings on her earlobes, how that dark freckle on her chest is shaped like Oklahoma. Eventually, her words blur together. You continue to feign attention, but your mind wanders: Do my bottom teeth show when I talk? Why is a male swan called a "cob?" If I had a twin, which one of us would be considered the "evil" one? Finally, you grow angry, first at yourself: Why am I still listening to this person? Then your anger shifts to the speaker, *Will you just shut the hell up!* You know you should say something, do something, but by this point you don't trust your own judgment. *Did I actually make that hanging motion, or just think it?*

The soup has given way to herb-encrusted salmon and warm goat cheese salad. When the server brought me my plate, this time I barely acknowledged her, partly because I was too busy talking, and mostly because I had appropriated more airs. This waitress was a member of the invisible working class, from which I was trying desperately to distinguish myself.

"Did you know Louise is a new grandmother?" Lady Headband abruptly changed the subject.

No, I did not know Louise was a new grandmother, I thought, feeling rebuffed. In fact, I didn't even know Louise, not that this mattered because Lady Headband had returned her attention to Amanda. "The baby's name is Harrison," she added. "Louise told me she practically has to pry him out of his mother's arms just to get a chance to hold him."

"I knew Amy and Stu had been trying for quite some time," Amanda said, which struck me as none of her business.

I ate my salmon while the two women gossiped. Louise. Amy. Stu. Baby Harrison. Whoever these people were, they clearly had no use for me.

"Louise calls Harrison her miracle grandbaby," Marion added.

Ah, an opening.

"One time when I was a ghostwriter for an obstetrician," I piped up, "I helped him write a book all about his work with women who want to have intercourse and make babies, but they have this condition called *vaginismus* . . ."

It's funny how particular words in certain social settings seem to project at a higher acoustic intensity, "vaginismus" being the perfect example. As soon as the word left my mouth, it seemed to catch the ear of my seatmates across the table, none of whom previously had been paying any attention to me.

"The incidence rate of vaginismus is actually quite high." I decided to forge ahead because, really, what choice did I have? Once a train has derailed, you just have to ride it out. "In fact, vaginismus is as common as erectile dysfunction!"

The two-hundred-year-old woman across the table raised her scribbled eyebrows.

"Fortunately," I reassured her, "with new treatment options, there is a cure."

Our hostess, thank goodness, chose that moment to tap a handheld microphone. All chairs turned to face her standing at her table. How had I gotten myself into this mess? I thought. All I had wanted to do was to convince Lady Headband and the others that I was a somebody, yet somehow I had ended up talking about sexual dysfunctions.

The hostess gave a short speech, thanking us for our contribution to the arts. "Through your individual and collective efforts, you have made our community a better place to create, to work, and to live," she raised her glass. We followed suit in a toast to ourselves. While it should have been obvious all along, I understood now that I had not been invited to this luncheon because I was a writer, a realm in which I constantly sought validation, but because I rented a space from our hostess so I could teach writing.

Chairs scraped again, and we turned our attention to dessert. I vowed to focus on my crème brulé and make only short, appropriate remarks. Or maybe just keep my mouth shut altogether.

Someone at the table raised the subject of quilts, specifically quilts that could be donated for a silent auction to raise money for an after-school arts program. Quilts were an easy subject for me to remain silent about, having grown up in Amish farm country. Since childhood, I have associated quilts with the smell of manure, and no amount of crafts-manship can change that.

"Any other fundraising ideas?" Amanda raised the question.

"How about a bake sale?" someone called out.

"Or we could do a community spelling bee," another volunteered.

My experience with fundraising was nil, given I avoided committee work like the plague. But then I realized I did have a suggestion, a good one, and best of all it involved my best celebrity author story. Here was a chance to redeem myself and name drop at the same time.

"A few years ago," I started, "I was invited to participate in a library fundraiser in Florida. Patrons of the library organized dinner parties where donors could mingle with well-known writers . . ."

Lady Headband touched my arm lightly.

"Excuse me," she placed her napkin on the table. "I'm afraid I need to run to another appointment." As if on cue, the others quickly followed suit. One of the women made a point to help our two-hundred-year-old seatmate from her chair, lest her infirmity inhibit her escape. In what seemed like seconds, the table was cleared.

But wait! Wait! I wanted to cry out. I hadn't even gotten to the good part of my story, the part about Khaled Hosseini, the best-selling author of *The Kite Runner* and other noteworthy novels. At the fundraiser, Khaled and I had been assigned to the same table. After we had mingled with donors, we wandered to the far side of the swimming pool to smoke and chat. "Who would have thought," I would have said to my seatmates, shrugging with self-deprecation, "me bumming a cigarette from Khaled Hosseini. And I don't even smoke!"

If Lady Headband had stuck around, she would have found this last comment amusing. Then I would have assured her that Khaled was as good-looking in person as he is on his book jackets. He also was a very nice man and we got along well, and even stayed in touch for a few years after the event. We're not *super* good friends, I would have confessed, given that he had probably forgotten me by now, but I do have his private home number. But I never got the chance to say any of this because the luncheon was over. My table was deserted, with no one left to impress but me and the fucking No Show.

I gathered my purse and gym bag and then headed to the ladies' room to change for the gym. If I hurried, I could still make it to my exercise class if I drove there directly. I was half changed when I realized I had forgotten to bring a T-shirt or sneakers. Oh well. I would go to class anyway, clearly in need of endorphins now more than ever.

As I was walking to my car, a woman called my name.

"Yes?" I thought her face was vaguely familiar, though I had no idea who she was.

"I went to your reading at the bookstore last month," she said. "I just wanted to say how much I enjoy your work."

"Thank you. Really, thank you." This was exactly the kind of attention I lived for, a stranger stopping me in the street to say how much she appreciated my writing. But not now, I thought. Not when I was wearing a stained bib with sweatpants and strappy sandals.

She headed off in the opposite direction, while I continued to totter my way down the street. So that was that, I thought. My one and only fan would forever assume I dressed like a crazy person. Meanwhile Lady Headband didn't even know my Khaled Hosseini story. But of course now she had an author story of her own, which would likely go something like this:

"The other day I was at a luncheon for women in the arts," I could just hear her saying this to her friends, all of them wearing tortoiseshell headbands with pointy teeth. "There was this dreadful writer seated next to me with soup spilled down her front." Here, she would dismiss me with a wave of her blue-blooded hand. "I can't recall her name, but what I do remember is that she just went on and on about some kind of dreadful sexual dysfunction . . ."

Spirit Animal Tricks

Every morning my friend Betsy starts her day by pulling a spirit animal card from her well-worn deck. Knowing your spirit animal, she explains, gives you insights on how to improve your life. It clarifies your power and purpose. These creatures of the wild provide protection, guidance, and healing. Betsy does alright for herself. She looks like she could be in an ad for eyeglasses that make you look pretty, intelligent, and from Ohio, all of which describe her perfectly. Life has thrown Betsy some serious curves, yet she exudes a contagious optimism, which makes me believe her spirit animals must know what they are doing.

One morning Betsy and I met for coffee at a trendy café, its air purified by a plethora of soft ferns and herbal elixirs. A product shelf displayed CBD oils and creams, candles to inspire healing and passion, and—not surprisingly—spirit animal cards for sale, though the café also provided a free deck for their customers to use. It turns out, however, that Betsy packs her own deck. She pulled it from her roomy bag and told me to cut the cards.

"The elk!" she exclaimed after revealing my spirit animal for that day. "The elk is an earth sign. It represents strength and stamina."

"Yes." I found myself nodding in approval. While I have never put much stock into astrology, I can relate to earth signs much more than my own birth sign, Pisces, a water symbol that does not align at all with my deadline-driven personality, my insistence on punctuality (If the invitation reads seven p.m. then show up at least five minutes early!), and my preference for breathing without the need for scuba gear. I like my feet firmly planted on the ground.

The elk on the card and I studied one another. It looked powerful and paternalistic, its kind eyes seemed to sympathize with my deepest thoughts: it's okay if you aren't always a perfect person, like right now, pretending that you believe in spirit animal cards. My lack of faith aside, the elk's steady gaze made me feel comforted and safe, feelings that I had been missing lately. While it has been years since I lost my parents, there are times I still feel like a bereft, albeit middle-aged orphan. Who will take me in if I can't pay my mortgage? Who will drive me to the mall to accommodate my faltering night vision? Who will tell me that the horror of pandemics, and rising sea levels, and mass shootings are grown-up problems, so it's okay if I just want to forget about everything and go to sleep between them in their big, safe bed?

"When in balance, the elk represents endurance, patience, and solid relationships," Betsy continued reading from the guidebook that accompanied the cards. "When out of balance, the elk must be sure to pace itself and take breaks."

I was surprised by how much the elk's guidance resonated with me, as if it knew just what I needed to hear. Until the elk came along, I had been feeling guilty for visiting with Betsy in the middle of what was supposed to be a workday, not to mention paying fourteen dollars for a foamy green drink that didn't even include alcohol. But now this strong and wise creature had assured me that I should take breaks to invest in relationships, just like I was doing with Betsy. For a moment, I fantasized about getting an elk as a pet. I could keep it in my tiny backyard at my condo and press my cheek against its warm coat and scratch it behind its antlers.

After that meeting, Betsy—with the exuberance of a New Age missionary—started pulling a spirit animal card for me most mornings and texting me the result. Yesterday, she told me that my spirit animal for the day was the owl. At least I think it was an owl. I don't remember, but what I do remember is that whatever the animal told me, it felt comforting and made a lot of sense at the time. Betsy also has pulled for me a starfish, a tiger, an otter, and an earthworm! (The latter was alarming, until I learned that spirit animals go deeper than their obvious traits, like the importance of their poop to our ecosystem.) I truly appreciate Betsy's efforts on my behalf, but usually the clarity and comfort these spirit animals inspire quickly abates, and the rest of the day I am left trying to recall which animal said what when. Is today the day I am in a period of transformation . . . or in touch with the infinite divine? Am I supposed to wait before making that big decision . . . or step out of my comfort zone?

I used to think I had a preponderance of peculiar friends, or at least peculiar to me given so many of them have faith in things that just don't resonate with my own weltanschauung. There is lovely Betsy, with her travel pack of spirit animals, not unlike Susan, a retired therapist who now keeps her own counsel, often with the help of an invisible bird on her shoulder. My friend Carol gave up a career in the law to study astrology and do tarot readings. Cheryl, a cancer researcher, found comfort after a devastating loss by becoming a medium. Frances, an energy healer, relies on her angels who speak to her through a psychic reader. And, to the surprise of no one, most of these same friends, treasures to a one, also swear by the power of crystals.

"Citrine!" One, or maybe all of these friends have proselytized. "It's just what you need to move your life forward. Plus, it will take care of any bladder issues!"

Spiritually speaking, I don't know what I believe in— certainly not the dogma of traditional religions, and, while I hate to admit it to my friends, or even to myself, I am also skeptical about most of the secular shortcuts to a mystical realm. But one thing I do know for sure is that I do not want bladder issues. With that in mind, I went out and bought myself a citrine necklace at a psychic fair held in our local town hall. The stone hangs from a natural hemp cord. It does look pretty; I'll say that much for it.

"TODAY I PULLED THE WHALE CARD FOR YOU!" Betsy texted me earlier this morning. "WHALES ARE ASSOCIATED WITH CREATIVITY!"

"OMG, THE WHALE IS PERFECT FOR TODAY," I texted back, and just like that I felt inspired to create something, anything! I read the description of the whale that Betsy had provided.

"With the whale spirit animal, there is a need for healing both physically and emotionally. Rely on your inner strength to navigate emotional depths." As with all my spirit animals for the day, the whale's message seemed perfectly timed. I do need to rely on my own healing powers—my own inner strength—to fix whatever is out of balance with me and not wait around for others to plumb my emotional depths. Could there be any better guidance for a middle-aged orphan, or for anyone, really, living with the weight of this world we live in today?

In the past Betsy has offered to give me my own deck of spirit animal cards, but I always turn her down. With my own psychic abilities, I could see myself stashing the deck in the closet where I have abandoned other whims and curios, including an old Ouija board from a lifetime ago. I don't believe in Ouija boards even more than I don't believe in spirit animal cards. Nevertheless, the thought of corralling these well-meaning animals into a cramped space alongside a game reputed to be a portal into Hell just feels wrong. I imagined the epic battles that would ensue—*Laydeeze and Gentlemen. Tonight's bout pits the reigning champ Beelzebub, Demon of Darkness, against the playful and inventive Otter, who reminds us to celebrate the simple things and embrace our inner child.*

If only I was a true believer in these spirit animals. If only I didn't feel like such a fraud. Illogical as it may sound, I worry that, if I don't believe in spirit animals, then who am I to waste their time? Even worse, because I know spirit animals are a deeply meaningful tradition in Indigenous and other cultures, it can make my dabbling in them feel like a form of cultural appropriation, like treating someone's totem as a kind of animal trick.

I wish I knew of a spiritual path that made sense to me—one that could light my way, even during the darkest hours—but I do know that I have come to appreciate the power of Betsy's well-worn deck. A card is pulled, and the elk presents itself, symbolizing strength and stamina. Another day, another card, the whale shows up, presuming I have inner strength, and who am I to argue with a 130,000-pound cetacean?

Maybe this is how faith foments? Maybe this is the deeper wisdom that these spirit animals have been trying to impart. It doesn't matter that I can't recall which animal told me to do what on any given day, or that I think of some of these creatures as pets, or that one day I am likely to cram all of them into a closet full of demons. Maybe that's not how the spirit world works. If these animals really do symbolize the elements—earth, water, fire, and air—then they are always up there or out there, supporting us, warming us, sustaining our every breath, whether we believe in them or not. What a beautiful concept, to think that faith does not have to flow both ways—to think that it doesn't matter whether I believe in spirit animals because they still believe in me.

Like a Punch to the Kidneys

"I'm not going to give him a kidney if he can't even call me on my birthday."

My friend Deb tells me this over dinner. She is talking about her brother, who is on dialysis, and who is also clearly on Deb's shit list because he didn't bother to call her on her last birthday. Apparently this brother, Bobby, thinks the kidney deal is as good as done, but Deb plans to set him straight.

"I told him I'd be *tested* to see if I was a match," Deb explains. "But that's a long way from agreeing to be his donor. And now I don't even feel like doing that. Let his wife give him one of her kidneys."

Well now. I can't say I blame Deb. It's rude not to wish a family member a happy birthday, especially if you want her kidney. I bet brother Bobby will be kicking himself when he finds out why Deb changed her mind. I bet Bobby's wife will be kicking him, too.

"All you had to do was pick up the phone," I can hear his wife whisper-yelling at him above the hush of the machines at the dialysis center. "But no, you couldn't be bothered and now I have to give you an organ."

Deb's comment continues to prickle at me. Donating a kidney is a really big deal. It can save a life—in Deb's case her own brother's life—and if Bobby can't come up with an alternative match he'll have to go on the national kidney transplant list where there is at least a five-year wait. Given the stakes, it surprised me that Deb could be so capricious about the issue, as if her sibling was simply asking her if she would lend him her car. "No way, Bobby, not after the last time when you left me with an empty tank."

All the more reason I found myself intrigued by Deb's way of weighing this issue. It made me realize that a spare kidney wasn't just a vital organ; it was something one could wield or withhold depending on your grudges and whims. A kidney was something you could leverage to your advantage. It was a form of power, pure raw power, and best of all, I realized, I had two of them.

Like many people, I have fantasized what I would do if I won the lottery. I know I would buy a jacuzzi tub and pay off my Toyota and hire someone to clean my condo with such enthusiasm that they could convince me I was actually doing them a favor. I also might go on a luxury safari, though I am afraid of animals in the wild, plus what if people thought I meant the *killing* kind of safari, which would put me in the worst possible company. Mostly, however, my lottery fantasies involve me spending my rich days either bestowing monetary gifts to people I like or, conversely, not giving money to people I don't like, even though we both know I could if I wanted to. It is unlikely I will ever win the lottery, so I doubt I will ever have the kind of expendable income that can change lives, or even earn me a place on the donor page of a playbill for regional theater. But what Deb has made me realize is that I already have something in my possession even more valuable than money. I have the gift of life.

What should I do with my spare kidney? Who might be the benefactor of my kindheartedness? Ever since I realized I had something of such value inside my body—How could I have not recognized this sooner?—I have spent considerable time imagining how I might wield this power to not only spare someone the draining experience of dialysis, but likely extend their life for a decade. The first benefactors who came to mind, naturally, are my two daughters, now in their twenties.

"My darling child," I imagine myself saying to one or the other, depending on which girl is my favorite at the moment. "I am bestowing you with one of my kidneys."

"Your kidney? I don't want your kidney," my chosen child would respond. "My own kidneys work just fine." It is true, in real life my daughters' kidneys are fully functioning (knock on wood, knock on wood, knock on wood), and in this fantasy scenario their kidneys, indeed all their organs, remain perfectly intact, otherwise it would take all the fun out of this mental exercise. Still, isn't it just like kids to think they know better than their parents.

"Take the kidney," I insist, waving away my favorite child's arguments. I could do without her tone but of course good parenting is all about picking your battles. "Do you know there are more than one-hundred thousand people on the kidney waitlist? Do you know how lucky you are to have a mother willing to have elective surgery for you?" I imagine my girl posting a photo of the two of us on Instagram after the successful transplant. We are holding hands in our side-by-side hospital beds, both looking in good color and well rested because the surgeon was willing to throw in an eye lift for me.

"I really don't want your kidney so please stop trying to give it to me," my now second-favorite child repeats. She can be so obstinate, just like when she insisted she did not want me to call her by her baby nickname in public, or chaperone her middle school dances, or correct her high school essays, and I am a professional editor!

"Fine," I snap. "I'm sorry you're too good to be seen with your mother's kidney. Maybe I'll give it to your sister!"

"I'm sorry, Mommy," she adds to soften her rejection.

Mommy. I used to love when my girls called me that. When did they get so grown up? When did I become that desperate mother who can't let go? It is time to imagine a different beneficiary, one who doesn't remind me that I and my spare organs remain an embarrassment to my children.

"Honey, I have decided to give you my spare kidney." In this scenario, I am snuggled up next to Helmut, who is watching a soccer game he recorded on his iPad. I am not worried this imagined scenario will end like the one with my favorite child because Helmut and I have an adult relationship as partners for nine years; there is nothing to navigate between us as tricky as the mother-daughter dynamic.

"Sounds good," Helmut says. "I'll keep that in mind if I ever need it." One of Helmut's many good qualities is his ability to easily follow my flights of imagination.

I take his hand, no, both of his hands in mine. It feels weird, like we are on *The Bachelorette*, but this is a life-and-death conversation that requires his undivided attention. "I think it will bring us even closer," I tell Helmut. "You'd do the same for me, right?"

"Of course," he says, side-eyeing the soccer game. "But first we'd need to get tested. Just to make sure we're a good match?"

I drop his hands. "Never mind," I snap. "Forget I ever offered. Why would you want my boring, old kidney anyway?" I know that Helmut—or rather the Helmut I have created in this scenario—was talking about testing to make sure our blood type and antibodies are compatible for a transplant. But sometimes a kidney is not just a kidney, and this imaginary Helmut has tapped into one of my most niggling secret worries—that we are no longer a good match as partners.

From my perspective, Helmut has maintained all the qualities that attracted me to him in the first place. He remains romantic and thoughtful, curious and conversant, fit and well groomed. In contrast, the past nine years have brought a steady desquamation of my own energy and attributes, which seem to be aging in dog years. I hesitate to think what it would be like if our kidneys were to meet now for a first date.

"Tell me about yourself?" Helmut's sexy kidney would ask my dumpy kidney seated next to him at the bar. While both our kidneys are, well, kidney shaped, I notice that his sits straighter than mine.

"What's there to tell," my own kidney responds with a heavy sigh. "I've been having a lot of issues with digestion. Plus, my back is killing me. And do you think the bartender could turn down this music?"

We chat for a spell, Helmut's kidney sharing its interests in music and art, while mine talks about taking on a class-action suit against big pharma, defending a man who murdered his wife, and pursuing opposition research on a political candidate. Too late, my kidney realizes it's describing season two of *The Good Wife*, which it binge-watched last Tuesday when it was supposed to be working.

"I'll be right back," my kidney says, heading to the restroom, the one place it still feels strong and capable, at least when it comes to passing waste as urine. Only recently it read an article where a noted transplant surgeon was quoted as saying that even if living donors are seventy, their kidneys can still save lives. My own kidney is buoyed by such reassuring news that, according to this surgeon, it is still a babe.

As my kidney walks to the restroom, it can feel Helmut's kidney checking out its backside. For a moment, my kidney wishes it had worn something other than its favorite brown corduroy pants, appropriately nicknamed "saggy baggies." But then again, my kidney shrugs, these pants are so comfortable that last night it wore them to bed.

The time had come to imagine yet another route to donation. Rather than giving my spare kidney to loved ones who no longer need me or who might discover that I am no longer a good match, I will give it to a fortunate stranger. This will put me in the category of one of those good Samaritans whose altruism not only saves the life of an unknown recipient, but may even inspire a chain of donations, depending on whether the first recipient has a committed donor who is willing to pay it forward to others in need of a transplant.

I play out this newest fantasy in my mind. A few weeks after successfully undergoing the removal of my kidney, I envision myself seated at my favorite café, feeling beatific as I watch the passersby out the window. I wonder, is the recipient of my spare body part that attractive woman with the adorable dog? Or maybe my kidney went to that white-haired gentleman who now, thanks to me, will live long enough to see his grandchildren graduate from college. I feel a sentimental tug at the site of my imaginary incision, the scar barely noticeable, even with my pallid skin tone.

A woman enters the café, blabbing loudly on her cell phone. "And then I said, it's none of your business what I do over my lunch break . . ." She pauses her conversation just long enough to ask the server for a latte. The sound of her voice is grating, and her one-way conversation disrupts my pleasant musings.

What if she was the beneficiary of my kindness? The thought annoys me. I reassure myself that, most likely, my kidney was put on ice and flown to a hospital in another part of the country. Maybe Baltimore or Cleveland or Amherst. Yes, Amherst. I would like my kidney to be somewhere that enjoys the seasons. But what if my kidney did go somewhere, or to someone I don't like? What if it went to a gorilla poacher, or a cheating spouse, or a close talker? I don't like the idea of relinquishing my one spare kidney to just anyone. There would need to be conditions, I decide. A lot of conditions given all the places and people I don't like.

Suddenly, the game of trying to envision a recipient for my spare kidney feels like it has played itself out, with me coming out as the loser. At first I had felt empowered, imagining what I would do with this gift of life. But what fun is an imaginary game when the reality is that I actually could donate a kidney to a stranger; except it would come with conditions. People—people just like me only with more charitable fortitude—do this on a regular basis. You fill out a form. You have the procedure. And, as one young man—the son of one of my close friends—reported after he actually did volunteer one of his kidneys to a stranger, "The fact is, it's awful to need a kidney, and it's really not that hard to give one."

My mind returns to my conversation with my friend Deb, whose brother Bobby is on dialysis. While I have never met Bobby, my imaginative powers make it easy to picture him resting in a recliner under a blanket, his blood flowing from his arm through a tube into a machine where it will be filtered for the next four hours.

Beep. Beep. Beep.

The room is filled with a row of patients all resting in identical recliners, all undergoing identical procedures. "How about you?" Bobby points to me squatting behind a ficus tree in the corner. "How about you give me—or any of us—one of your kidneys?"

I know what I should say. I know what I should do. Instead, I can only envision myself shaking my head no, then looking away because I don't want to see their faces, which probably look like they've all been punched in the kidneys, no humor intended. Indeed, these imagined scenarios have made it painfully clear that I am not the type to simply volunteer a vital organ; to give the gift of life to someone in need, at least without petty conditions. You could say this reflects a moral weakness on my part, or exposes a lack of generosity and empathy, but given my inclination toward making up fantasies, I prefer to just call it a failure of imagination and leave it at that.

Recalculating, Recalculating, Recalculating . . .

"Start out going northeast . . ." This is the first instruction the GPS lady with the Australian accent says to me as I venture out of my driveway to head to a restaurant in Concord, New Hampshire, located a mere ninety minutes from my house. *Northeast?* I don't know how they do things in Australia, but does this GPS lady think I carry a compass around with me? Does she assume I have completed some kind of orienteering program with the Boy Scouts? I have absolutely no idea which way is northeast. When it comes to directions, my brain only registers "left" and "right" and even then, I have to use a mnemonic to tell them apart: *I write with my right hand.*

Luckily, I have lived in the same place for over twenty-five years, which is why I know enough to turn left out of my driveway to hit the entrance to the interstate. Already, I am tense. I meant to leave a half-hour early, but then circumstances (trying and failing to find my naughty cat, Kitty, who managed to slip outside) left me with just the relegated 1.5 hours needed (according to my GPS lady) to cover the distance required. This means that, in all likelihood, I will be late because I don't like to pass on a curve and because I have a medical condition, albeit one mostly overlooked by the AMA. My condition? *Directionally disabled*—no hyperbole intended. Who hasn't heard comments like these a million times:

"I suck at directions."

"I can't find my way out of a paper bag."

People say things like this all the time. I know mental impairments aren't a contest, but I doubt anyone else in the whole wide world has logged the hours I have spent lost and confused, directionally speaking. I am hopeless when driving to new places, but equally hopeless when close to home. When I exit one of the two busy shopping plazas in town, for example, I have a knack for turning in the opposite direction of wherever I am headed, forcing me to sit through a series of ill-timed traffic lights before I can fix my mistake. Just the other day my daughter asked me to meet her at her workplace, where I have dropped her off plenty of times when we shared a car.

"It's on the same road as the post office," she reminded me when I asked her for detailed directions. "*The post office.* You pass it almost every day."

I also have driven endless, unmarked Vermont backroads, not for pleasure but because I was frantically disoriented and out of cell-service range. Out of desperation, I have knocked on more than one door of some remote dwelling, seeking help to find my way home. By all accounts, I should be the subject of one of those unsolved mysteries shows: *How did this woman's decapitated head end up seventy miles from her house, when she was only going to the liquor store three miles away?*

And the problem is no less acute when I'm on foot. When I was six, my parents moved us to a new house, an average-sized suburban home, and the first night I fell into a panic when I couldn't find my way from the bathroom back to my bedroom. Years later, I took my firstborn in her stroller for a walk in this same childhood neighborhood and got lost on the return home (thanks in part to all the new development). Once I needed to elicit help from a security officer because I couldn't find my car in a parking garage, only to eventually discover I wasn't even looking in the right garage. And the first (and last) time I participated in a 10K trail run a few years ago I got so turned around in the woods that the organizers had to send rescuers to find me.

Would you like to know two of the scariest words in the English language for someone like me? Corn maze.

Now, as I motor down the interstate toward Concord, I try to relax, despite my directional disability, and the fact that I don't like leaving the house without finding my cat. Still, this isn't the first time Kitty has spent the day outdoors, so why not hope for the best. It's a nice, sunny day. My car, Sparkles, is all gassed up. And I still have an hour on the interstate before confronting any potential wrong turns that might await me after Exit 2. The friend I am meeting has reassured me that the restaurant he's chosen for us is right off the exit.

"You can't miss it," he promised.

If I had a nickel . . .

On the spectrum of disabilities, I figure the absence of any sense of direction should elicit at least the same degree of sympathy as, say, color blindness. No one deserves to be judged for wearing mismatched clothing, or failing to distinguish ketchup from chocolate sauce, nor should anyone be judged for not knowing north (or, worse yet, *northeast*) from a hole in the ground. It gets old, enduring the reactions of others who don't understand that this condition is really a thing, and not just a matter of me being scatterbrained.

More problematic than how others respond to my condition, however, is my own reaction to my disability, which usually takes the form of a hissy fit whenever I find myself lost, whether in the car or on foot. After all these years, I know I should be more accepting, even philosophical about my condition. I remember once reading a quote by Helen Keller: "I thank God for my handicaps. For through them I have found myself, my work, and my God." That sentiment speaks to just one noteworthy difference between me and Helen Keller, though I do recognize how my cognitive deficit has made me a better writing teacher. When someone just can't grasp a writing tenet—such as how the phrase *her eyes roamed the room* is not only cliched but instantly evokes the image of two anthropomorphized eyeballs pacing a room like they're proctoring an exam—I understand that student's struggle. Similar to how I have tried to teach myself to compensate when finding my way around the world, I know how to help others navigate the page, even if they lack an ear for language.

Still, beyond the empathy my disability has engendered for struggling writers, I have yet to find a reason to be thankful for the countless times I went the wrong way.

Exit 2 looms closer and closer. A memory pops into my head, yet another directional misadventure I haven't thought of in ages. This one took place in my late twenties when, for a brief interlude, I was dating two men simultaneously, both graduate students in psychology. It seemed like an odd coincidence—to fall for two men studying mental health—or maybe not. At the time, I was working at an advertising agency where I spent most of my endless workdays writing copy for a nationally known weight-loss program, each headline a variation on the same theme:

"Arlene Lost 27 Pounds and 12 Inches and Found Happiness!"

"Sheila Said Goodbye to 3 Dress Sizes in 3 Weeks!"

"Beverly 'Relaxed Away' 43 Pounds. No Sweat!"

With no semblance of fulfillment or meaning derived from my work, what could be more romantically appealing than a boyfriend with an air of gravitas, significant student debt, and a frameless bed ringed with stacks of paperbacks by famous thinkers and philosophers (Jung! Nietzsche! Kierkegaard!). This described budding psychologist number one, Steve, whom I dated for a year, until he left for a PhD program halfway across the country. Given the circumstances, we agreed to try to visit each other every few months, but money was tight, and we found ourselves unhappy with a long-distance relationship but unwilling to call it quits.

It was at the end of that first year in love limbo with Steve that I met budding psychologist number two, Joe, who had almost completed the requirements of his doctoral program in forensic psychology and was working as a prison counselor while preparing for his final oral exams. Joe was not shy about his feelings for me, so I certainly liked that about him, but did I like him enough to date him? Would this be cheating on Steve? Or would it be stupidity, to close myself off to new relationship possibilities? For a couple months Joe and I met up for drinks at a bar near my house, but my ambivalence kept things casual. Then one night he came over to my place, bringing with him notecards he had prepared to help him study for his orals.

—What are death-qualified jurors?

—Contrast an advocacy brief and a science-translation brief.

—Which of the following is not a characteristic of psychopathy?
   a. Impulsivity
   b. Pathological lying and motivation
   c. Overwhelming guilt and remorse
   d. A continual willingness to violate social norms

I was in love. Or at least my feelings shifted considerably that evening. Despite having a semi-boyfriend halfway across the country, how could I not feel attracted to a man well studied in pathological lying, yet still willing to socialize with me. Later that evening over beers, I confided to Joe something I had rarely told anyone.

"I want to be a writer," I confessed. "Maybe write a book or something," I added, already feeling foolish.

"That sounds cool," Joe said.

In retrospect, I recognize that his response was a normal follow-up. In my head, however, I think that the reaction I had expected from him, from anybody at that time, was something more in line with a calling out of my audacity. *"Chapter 1: Wendy lost 23 pounds and 17 inches and now she thinks she can be a writer. What a joke."*

A few weeks later, Joe asked me if I wanted to go with him to a Foreigner concert, but he wanted to know if I could meet him at his apartment, which was closer to the venue. Until this point, I had never been to his place, primarily because it was a thirty-minute drive from my apartment, and was I really that invested? But after our last date, I was starting to see Joe not just as a forensic psychologist with interesting notecards, but as a potential boyfriend rather than a placeholder.

"I live in the apartment complex by the King of Prussia Mall," Joe told me. Same exit, but go past the mall, then take a left, then a right, then . . ." With no GPS, I scribbled frantically, knowing I'd need to rely on detailed directions. "You won't have any trouble finding it," he assured me, but Joe's training was in profiling criminals lacking moral, not directional, compasses.

Usually when I am motivated to find my way somewhere I eventually get there but not this time. So many routes: 76, 276, 23! Then Old Gulph Road, New Gulph Road, plus more turns that made no sense once I got myself twisted around. An hour later I was crying and explosive and already embarrassed as I imagined trying to explain to Joe my ineptitude. Eventually, I gave up and somehow found my way back to my apartment.

"It sounds like you were really close," Joe said, when I phoned him later. "You couldn't have been more than a mile away." His voice was neutral. Did he believe me when I told him how I had gotten lost? Or did he suspect I had blown him off—my no-show another manifestation of my earlier ambivalence about our relationship? "I'll catch you next time I'm out your way," he offered, but he never followed up, nor did I ever contact him. I think in my thwarted efforts to reach Joe's house I had crossed (and recrossed, and circled back, and recrossed again) some Rubicon of humiliation.

Now, over three decades later, my GPS lady instructs me in her Aussie accent to take Exit 2 and turn right, my destination a mile farther on the left. Within minutes I see the restaurant ahead, and what looks like a large patio of outdoor seating. Relief! My lunch date was correct: you can't miss this place, except apparently you can miss the entrance because I drive right past it, not realizing it is the left *before*, not in front of, the restaurant.

I imagine the moment of my conception—gamete one hooking up with gamete two, then moments later they have their first spat. "You brought the chromosome for directional skills, right?" the egg asks the sperm.

"What?" the sperm gives his mate that look that makes her want to box his ears. "I thought you were in charge of directions!"

This is a joke I once made up to mock my own disability, though it never struck me as funny. Now, driving home from my lunch date, it still fails to amuse me, though I can't help but laugh at the memory of my friend waving me down from the restaurant's outdoor seating area after I'd finally managed to circle my way back to the entrance.

I flip the visor in my car to shield me from the glare of the sun. It's a straight shot home, no more stress, no need to worry. I regret now, like I always do, the rush of panic I felt when I missed that last turn to the restaurant, followed by an eruption of anger at myself, my stupidity, the stupidity of illogically placed entrances. When I did arrive fifteen minutes late, my friend hadn't made any fuss about my tardiness. We'd had a good visit, once I'd settled myself down.

After so many years dealing with this disability, I know I need to find a way to be more accepting of it. Yes, my condition has inconvenienced me almost daily, adding an undercurrent of anxiety to even the most routine outings. My disability is also the stuff of many of my nightmares, manifesting in iterations of me failing to escape from somewhere because I don't know which way to run, or failing to save a loved one in need because I don't know how to reach them. But those are just bad dreams, and, like all dreams, they can offer insight.

When I think back to decades ago when I was dating the two psychologists, it strikes me as noteworthy that the only other time I drove to the King of Prussia Mall was when I went there to shop for a wedding dress, about a year after my failed attempt to find Joe's apartment. By then, Steve and I, weary of our long-distance semi-relationship, had decided for a hastily arranged marriage, in part so that we wouldn't second-guess our decision. Less than a month after Steve's proposal, there I was at my small wedding, wearing a pretty ivory dress I had managed to find at the King of Prussia mall.

I thank God for my handicaps. For through them I have found myself, my work, and my God. Maybe, this is what Helen Keller was talking about, I thought, not just accepting your handicaps but appreciating what they have done for you. What if I hadn't been born with a directional disability? Then I might have found my way to Joe's place that evening I was to meet him. I might have found myself on an entirely different life path than the one I have actually been living.

But why would I want that? What part of my existing life would I be willing to give up? My kids? My marriage, which ended after twenty-five years, but how can you untangle the good parts from the bad? What is the point of dwelling in what-ifs, or roads not taken, or all those wrong roads? Plus, who is to say which road is the right one? What if I had found my way to Joe's place that night? Theoretically, I might be living in an apartment complex behind the King of Prussia Mall, having to listen to Foreigner albums for the rest of my life.

As I pull into my driveway, my GPS lady with the Australian accent announces, "You have arrived at your destination." I swear, I also hear her let out a heavy sigh. *Why do I have to get all the head cases,* I can just imagine her complaining to the other GPS voices. *Yoda and Darth Vader never get these wackos who can't tell their left from their right.*

On the stoop of my front door, my naughty cat circles my legs in greeting. "Don't you run away like that ever again." I pick up Kitty and scold her with kisses. We head inside, welcomed by a familiar messy row of shoes and other family touchstones. Kitty leaps on her snack chair, demanding a treat. Being a wanderer by nature, I am sure she has a far better sense of direction than me, but I'm just glad that both of us—one way or another—managed to find our way home.

⌒

The Seven-Year Bitch

A friend and I are having coffee around my kitchen island. She is gushing about her new romance, a man I have met only a few times.

"I told him I was going shoe shopping and he wants to go with me! Can you believe how sweet that is?"

I can believe it. For one thing, we're only talking about shoe shopping, not accompanying her to Wagner's "Ring" cycle, so I can't give him too many points. For another thing, this friend is awesome. She's a stunner, curious about the world, a "catch" to put it succinctly, though that is not exactly how I phrased it when I authored her profile for her on Match.com where she met this man. This woman and I have been close friends going on two decades, since our youngest children, now young adults, became buddies in preschool. Personality-wise, we have little in common, yet the friendship abides, somehow transcending my intermittent sociability (Stop by! Don't stop by!) and her horror at the way I drive.

"I love how he really listens to me," she continues to gush about her new man. "And he doesn't seem to have a lot of baggage, thank God. Plus, he's such a good kisser!"

I wonder: Is this how I sounded when I first started dating Helmut nine years ago? In terms of emotional effusiveness, I would say I am more of a ranter than a gusher, but who knows? Love does funny things.

What I do remember, clearly, is this friend's willing ear and protective instincts as my relationship with Helmut progressed, and how she offered her approval of him in monthly increments:

"Well, I like him a lot better than the last guy you were dating."

"He *seems* nice."

"You two look cute together."

"Helmut is a really lovely person."

"You are so lucky!"

"Does Helmut have a brother?"

Now nine years have somehow slipped by, and my friend is the one with the new romance, while I am the one sipping in judgment as we talk across my kitchen island. Thus far, her new man has earned my trust just enough to remove him from the category of potential serial killer, but whether he is good enough for her in the long run will require much more time and scrutiny.

Ping.

Ping.

Ping.

I catch her sneak yet another glance at her phone, which is practically throbbing on my kitchen counter with sweet and steamy texts, some of which she has previously shared with me.

"He wants to make us dinner tonight." She scrolls through his latest missives, flirtatiously tossing her hair, which is so thick and luxurious it deserves its own Match.com profile.

"I'll alert the media," I say.

"Sorry," she giggles and turns over her phone, returning her attention to our conversation. "But you remember how it was," she adds, "back when you and Helmut were first in love."

Infatuation. The Oxford Dictionary defines this noun as "very strong feelings of love or attraction for someone or something, especially when these are unreasonable and do not last long." Clearly, my friend and her new man are in the throes of infatuation, as I once was with Helmut. Now, however, according to my friend, that stage of my and Helmut's romance has apparently been relegated to the dusky past. *You remember how it was* . . . Her comment rankled, making me feel like my relationship with Helmut belonged at the old people's table at a wedding reception, the table furthest from the dance floor.

"Just look at those crazy kids." I envisioned a more wrinkled version of myself picking at my chicken cordon bleu, thinking I should have opted for the flounder. "In my day, we frowned upon social dancing."

"What did you say?" Helmut would cup one of his saggy ears toward me, his hearing a casualty of the Battle of Gettysburg.

You remember how it was . . . I know my friend did not intend anything by her comment. By its very definition, infatuation is a passing phase, and good riddance in some respects, because ideally once you get beyond the mushy, shoe-shopping phase, the relationship then evolves into a more substantive and enduring love. The problem is, I have never accepted this natural progression from infatuation to love, at least not for me and Helmut.

Helmut is my second "forever" relationship. (The first one being my marriage, which ended amicably after twenty-some years.) The difference this time around is that I want both phases—those unreasonably strong feelings *and* the more substantive love—and I want them both at the same time, for all our years of togetherness, until we die of old, old age at the exact same moment and the coroner must pry us apart from each other's cold, dead embrace. This was going to be the reality of my relationship with Helmut, and I was not going to let some dictionary definition put a shelf-life on any of my unreasonably strong feelings, especially when it came to love!

"Give me a proper kiss," Helmut had said this to me at the close of our first date. Nothing would have pleased me more, except that every time I went to kiss him, I broke out in nervous laughter. I was aware of his height, the stretch of his pink cotton shirt across his broad shoulders, the square toe of his cowboy boots. Earlier that evening—our knees brushing as we swiveled on our barstools—I had inventoried his features: sharp cheekbones, a trim beard, a smooth expanse of forehead. Maybe it was the intensity of his gaze or his German accent, but it struck me that he would make the perfect handsome extra in *Schindler's List*, albeit on the wrong side of history.

Later that night, I thought about a story Helmut had told me over our second round of cocktails. After he and his wife had split a few years earlier, Helmut had taken responsibility for their beloved cat, which was apparently huge and ailing and had to pee an inordinate number of times, but it refused to go outside. To accommodate the poor creature, Helmut mentioned that he kept five litter boxes in the basement of his house and had to change them at least twice a day. Five litter boxes! I thought, driving home after that first date. He already had me at four.

Helmut moved into my condo less than a year after that first date. The first time we went out I already had deigned him "The Perfect Boyfriend for Me." It was true then, and it is still true now, which makes what happened in year seven of our relationship even more of a mystery.

I fell out of infatuation.

Even as it was happening, even as I still recognized in Helmut everything that had attracted me to him in the first place—his dearness, his ridiculous amount of energy, his curiosity, his creative talents (cartooning, singing, playing piano!)—I could feel my unreasonable feelings of love and attraction fading away, then returning, only to fade again and become more and more elusive. To most outsiders, even to ourselves, I am sure we continued to look like the same couple we had always been—loving and in love. Only my newly infatuated friend (*You remember how it was . . .*) seemed to recognize the change in my relationship, but I guess when you are wearing infatuation goggles, it is easy to spot a fraud.

What happened in year seven between me and Helmut? The only thing I am sure of is that I am mostly to blame. (Though I also blame the government, the exorbitant cost of college tuition, my litigious neighbor, the local Toyota dealership, and the weather, even without the extremes of climate change.) With hindsight, I try to think of a specific incident, a reason I grew distant and angry but all that comes to mind are small moments.

"Tell me stuff." From the start, that was my invitation to
Helmut to share stories about his life, or to make up stories
about us. ("There once was a bear from the Black Forest who

fell in love with a white deer from across the ocean . . .") I loved how Helmut carried our conversations, affording me the luxury of simply listening. Then one day I thought, *Stop talking. I just want quiet.*

It is a gray fall morning and I make myself a mug of pumpkin spice coffee. Helmut offers to top it with steamed milk from our espresso machine. "Add a little nutmeg," I say. He returns my foamed coffee with cocoa powder on top. "Thanks," I manage, thinking, *What part of nutmeg don't you understand?*

I am in bed, tossing and turning, worrying about work, money, growing old, the strange bump on my forearm, my lack of hobbies, and the thought that if I do survive this strange bump on my forearm, I won't have anything to do when I am old because of my lack of hobbies. Plus, my car has died and cannot be fixed. Helmut's car, by contrast, works just fine, but his is a standard and I only know how to drive automatic. Next to me, Helmut is listening to music through earbuds, his head bopping along. He reaches out an arm, inviting me, as usual, to lie closer. I turn my back and curl around my anger. *I bet Helmut likes that I can't drive his car, that way he doesn't have to worry about all my hard braking.*

Our seven-year anniversary arrives, and we are having a drink at the same bar, sitting on the same barstools where our knees touched during our first date. This time my knees, like sentinels, face straight ahead. "What's the matter?" Helmut asks. "Nothing's the matter," I say. I stir my cocktail, keenly aware of the distance I have created between us. *This is the worst kind of loneliness, when you feel lonely, and you are not even alone.*

At some low point during year seven, when I was tempted to give it all up, I had taken to sleeping in our spare room, making up excuses at first—"I want to watch a movie in bed, and don't want the light to disturb you." Soon enough, the wall between Helmut and me grew larger and larger in my mind, reminding me of the last year of my marriage when my husband and I shared a house but basically lived separate lives.

When I think about why that forever relationship ended, one seemingly insignificant memory comes to mind. I was sitting on the loveseat in our kitchen when I noticed that the heavy fan rotating over my head seemed precariously mounted on the ceiling. It looked like some bolts may have come loose. My husband came into the room.

"That fan doesn't look safe," I remarked, though I didn't muster the energy to move. "If it came down it could decapitate the person sitting beneath it."

My husband looked up, assessing the situation. "It wouldn't decapitate them," he commented, equally passive. "It would crush their skull."

After my husband and I announced our split, I remember the surprise among our friends and family. "You seemed so happy," they said. What happened?" I know I cannot pin my divorce on a single disagreement about a ceiling fan. But maybe after so many years of togetherness, the whole of these cumulative expenditures—*Why couldn't he just go along with decapitation?*—becomes greater than the sum of the good parts, at least if you let them.

Welcome to year nine of me and Helmut, and the return of my infatuation. I can't say for sure how this happened, other than the closer I got to losing Helmut, the more I realized that I was on the verge of ruining something wonderful, and for what reason? No reason, really, other than my own lifelong habits of erecting emotional walls, losing perspective, and taking people for granted.

When something isn't broken, it is hard to know how to fix it, yet as year seven unfurled, I also began to unfurl. Goodbye Seven-Year Bitch, I thought, reflecting on the nickname I had assigned myself. Don't let the door hit you on the way out.

This time around in my second forever relationship, I feel exactly the same, only different. I think when you are first infatuated with someone, you have no concept that those unreasonable feelings could ever end, so you are more susceptible to the thousands of tiny paper cuts that can erode them, like cocoa powder when you wanted nutmeg, or the fact that you can't drive a standard. But if you are lucky enough to become re-infatuated with the same person, then you not only carry forward those strong feelings of love and attraction, but also a perspective of how much can be lost.

You remember how it was . . . I do remember how it was, but here I am not recalling those first months when my relationship with Helmut was new, and the ping of every text had me flirting with my phone. Instead, I am remembering year seven, and seeing that year through the frame of an abacus—a calculation of missed kisses, hands not held, stories not told, kindnesses I denied. Everyone knows that the older we get the faster time passes. Why did I squander all those opportunities for love and attraction? Why did I risk Helmut's heart and my own?

In bed, Helmut reaches out an arm, inviting me, as usual, to lie closer. He is listening to music through his earbuds, his head bopping along. I curl in his direction and inventory his features for the umpteenth time: sharp cheekbones, a trim beard, a bit more forehead thanks to the passage of time.

I have seen photos of Helmut as a child and here is that same little boy with high color in his cheeks. Here is that man with an air of intensity who asked me for a proper kiss on our first date. Here, too, is the Perfect Boyfriend for Me, not just for now, but into the forever future. In my mind's eye I can see Helmut, a dear old man who is not allowed to die until the exact same moment that I do. You could call this an unreasonable feeling, but when it comes to infatuation the second time around, I think it makes perfect sense.

~

Why Cotton Mather Was a Hero

A Five-Paragraph Essay

Dear Cotton Mather,

I am eight years old and afraid of witches, just like you! I know they are real because at night I can see their shadows in my room, and I can hear them in my closet. Even when they are quiet I know they are there and will do something terrible to me if I come out from under the covers. Some nights I get so scared I yell for my mom to come get me so I can sleep between her and my dad. My sister, who is four years older than me and calls me "Warthog," (which tells you the kind of person she is) says that I am too old to believe in that baby stuff. But you are old and you believe in witches! And you are super smart! I know you went to Harvard when you were only twelve. Plus you were a famous minister back when people were Puritans and had to be really religious, and you published lots of books and articles.

    I know all this because my second-grade class just finished a unit on Colonial America, and everyone had to write a five-paragraph essay on something they learned. I wrote about you and the Salem witch trials in 1692. That year, fourteen ladies, five men, and two dogs got killed for being witches. (I was sad when I learned about the dogs.) All of them were hung except one man, Giles Corey, who was pressed under big rocks to make him say he was a witch, but that part didn't work. He just died two days later, and the only thing he said while he was being tortured was, "more weight."

When I did my research about you, the articles I read made it sound like you were the bad person and not the witches. I told my mom I was going to write my five-paragraph essay on you because I thought you were a hero to try to save the world from witches. She yelled at me like she yells at the TV. "Seriously? The guy's as awful as half the people in Congress today!" She was making a chocolate cake and when she lifted the electric mixer batter went flying all over the counter. "They're all just a bunch of right-wing blowhards who couldn't care less about helping people." Then my mom remembered she was yelling at me and not the news so she hugged me and used her sorry voice, "Honey, you can write about anything you want. This is still a free country. I hope."

Please don't be mad at my mom. She is an author like you, and nice most of the time. She is part of the reason I am sending you this letter because she told me that if I ever saw someone being bullied, I should stand up for that person, and not be quiet. (That was last year when I told her about some girls at school who kept hiding Bahir's lunch box, though her lunches are weird so maybe they were just trying to help her.) After the witch trials, people decided they didn't want to think about witches anymore, and they blamed you for all the people who got hung. One time someone even threw a bomb in your window, but that may have been because you told everyone they should get shots so they wouldn't die of smallpox. (Thanks a lot, Mr. Mather. Ouch!)

It made me feel bad that people got mad at you for believing in witches. I know how scary it is to know witches are out there, just waiting to get you and do terrible things. That's why I decided to send you my five-paragraph essay to show you that lots of people today would love you and be glad when you tell them you'll do whatever it takes to protect them from scary stuff.

Mr. Mather, I hope you like what I wrote. Oh, and sometimes in my essay I used your exact words, but my teacher, Ms. Hardwell, says that is not copying as long as I use quotation marks.

Cotton Mather was a hero because he wanted to find out why so many scary things kept happening to the Puritan people who had moved all the way from England to the Massachusetts Bay Colony so they could get away from evil. These scary things that happened included Indian attacks, freezing cold winters, and people fighting when they were supposed to be nice. Also, lots of normal children and grown-ups started acting crazy, screaming and twisting in circles, and foaming at the mouth. Other spooky things happened too, like the time a cat flew through an open window and tried to crush a man in his bed so he couldn't breathe. It turned out the cat was really the neighbor lady who was a witch and had just made herself look like a cat. This is a fact because the man in bed said it really happened to him. Cotton Mather told everyone things would stop being so scary, if they got rid of all the witches who were working for the devil.

Cotton Mather was a hero because he was not just an expert at being a minister, he was also a witch expert! One time there was a family called the Goodwin family with four children and no mother. The four children were well behaved until they started yelling and hitting and wouldn't do chores. Plus, they had terrible pains all over their bodies and barked. Cotton Mather figured out who was to blame. It was crazy Goody Glover, a poor lady who talked like the Irish, and who cleaned the Goodwins house and did their laundry. Crazy Goody Glover had put a spell on the children. She even said so herself at her trial before she was hung. Cotton Mather called Goody Glover a "hag" and an "Idolatrous Roman Catholic," and he wrote about her in his famous book called *Memorable Providences: Relating to Witchcraft and Possessions*. His book told about how he had saved the Goodwin children from Goody Glover, except for Martha, who was thirteen and could fly like a goose. To save her, Cotton Mather brought her to live with his family. One time he showed Martha the pages he was writing about her, but she threw them at his head. He wrote about her bad behavior and what she said to him, "And she particularly told me that I should quickly come to disgrace by that history."

Cotton Mather was a hero because he helped make sure no witches, not even the good ones, got away. In 1692, so many people in Salem got accused of being witches the jails got too full. It didn't matter if you were a mom or sister or best friend or went to church, anyone could be called a witch, even a homeless five-year-old kid! The judges in the witch trials didn't know who to believe and who to hang, but Cotton Mather helped them out by telling them that the real witches were "among the poor, and vile, and ragged beggars upon Earth." He also said that people who didn't believe in witches, or stood up for someone accused of being a witch, were really "witch advocates." This helped stop people from lying to protect their witch relatives and friends. In his famous book, Cotton Mather also told the judges to be careful about "spectral evidence," which meant that just because someone *said* they saw their wife or neighbor talking to the devil, that didn't always mean that person was a witch. But then he added this part, "Nevertheless," the best thing to do was have a "speedy and vigorous prosecution." With that extra part, Cotton Mather helped the judges make sure no witches would get away.

Cotton Mather was a hero because he helped destroy the leader of the witches! This was a man named George Burroughs, who was a Puritan minister just like Cotton Mather, only it turns out he was probably a Baptist and priest of the devil. At George Burroughs's trial, people told how they knew he was a witch because he survived Indian attacks when he should have been killed, and because his two dead wives had told them so after they were dead. He also was able to bite people during the trial, even though it looked like he was just sitting in a chair. Cotton Mather called George Burroughs a "very puny man." But then something weird happened. Right when George Burroughs was standing on the ladder about to be pushed off and hung, he said the Lord's Prayer without making any mistakes! This was impossible! Everybody knew a witch couldn't say the Lord's Prayer because Cotton Mather had told them so. So after George Burroughs got pushed off the ladder anyway, people started crying and feeling bad. The good thing was, Cotton Mather showed up right then on a big horse. He explained that just because George Burroughs could say the Lord's Prayer, that didn't mean he wasn't the leader of the witches. Sometimes the Devil could look like "an Angel of Light." That made everyone feel better, so they killed four more witches that day.

Cotton Mather was a hero because he knew he was right, no matter what anyone else told him. The Salem witch trials only lasted a year because people started being more afraid of being *called* a witch than having a witch put a spell on them. So they stopped tattling on each other and thought about their behavior. Some of the men on the jury, and even one of the judges, told the families of the dead witches they were sorry. But Cotton Mather never said he was sorry. The next year he wrote a new book called *More Wonders of the Invisible World* that said there were a lot more witches, and we should still be afraid of them. Hardly anybody liked the new book though, and nobody even thanked him for all the hard work he had done before to hunt down the other dead witches. I think this is wrong because Cotton Mather really tried to make people safe. If Cotton Mather was alive today I bet a lot of people would think he is a hero, and maybe even vote for him to be president, because he would know who to blame when bad things happen, and he would promise to kill all the scary witches trying to hurt them, including the ones in my closet.

The End

PS. My mom said she liked my essay a lot, especially the part where Martha Goodwin said you would come to disgrace and threw the pages of your book at your head. "Amen," my mom said. (You see, Mr. Mather, you're such a good minister you've even turned my mom religious!)

PPS. I think my sister is a witch.

FLAWSOME!

The print on the Zumba instructor's oversized, hot-pink tank top reads "FLAWSOME!" At first though I can't read it because, as a newbie to the class, I have positioned myself in the very back of the room, flush with a rack of kettlebells. Zumba, however, turns out to be a fiercely competitive sport, with the other first-timers and insecure types vying for the farthest real estate from the instructor and the wall-length mirror in the front. Before long, a deceptively pleasant-looking latecomer has wedged herself between me and the back wall. She throws an elbow, forcing me to shimmy forward. If only I knew how to shimmy.

FLAWSOME! Now I can read the bold print on the instructor's tank top.

"Don't worry if you can't follow the steps," the instructor cheers us on over a remix of "Uptown Funk." "There's no right or wrong in Zumba. It's all about letting loose and having fun." The instructor is a white, middle-aged woman, whose face I know I will forget the minute I leave class. This is because I suffer from a mild form of prosopagnosia, and also because she looks familiar in that way so many women in my small Vermont town vaguely resemble one another. Maybe she is the lady who makes me get on the scale every time I go to the doctor's office, which is almost as much of a disincentive toward wellness as the giant deductible on my health insurance. Maybe I have seen her at the farmer's market doling out free samples of her handcrafted goat cheese?

Maybe she took one of my writing workshops in the distant past, where I can promise you, I do not tell people to just let loose and have fun on the page, at least not after the first fourteen drafts.

The instructor slaps her thigh, indicating we are supposed to switch to something called the Merengue March, but her left is my right, plus the wall of backsides in front of me is blocking most of my view. (God, how I hate the word *athleisure*.) Already I am confused by the tricky steps and deflated by my lack of coordination. Still, I try my hardest to follow the footwork and arm waving. Toward the end of the hour, as I am dripping sweat from anxiety rather than exertion, I catch the eye of a dour, haggard blond woman in the mirror. To my shock, I realize, that woman is me.

So, it is only Zumba, right? Zumba is a calorie-burning fitness program set to Latin music and adaptable for people from ages two to one hundred, at least according to Wikipedia. What kind of an uptight bitch can't have fun in a class like that? You are reading her right now.

When I was a kid, I used to have wicked temper tantrums whenever I struggled with a task or tried to learn something new, and some things have not changed over the decades. Sure, you will no longer see my outside-self pounding my flutophone on the ruffled bedspread of my canopy bed because I cannot get the notes right to "Mary Had a Little Lamb," but my inside-self tells a different story. So many times, when I feel awkward or incompetent, whether it is because it takes me ten minutes to back my Toyota out of my narrow garage, or because an editor has rejected my work, my inside-self feels like reactor number two in Three Mile Island, circa 1979.

Over the years I have tried, tried, tried to change this aspect of myself. I want to be able to feel FLAWSOME, even when I fail. Especially when I fail, which is when I feel the most like, well, a failure. To move in this direction, I have sought the help of a few therapists for brief interludes, but it's hard to benefit from therapy when you spend the majority of your fifty-minute hour acting chipper as you exaggerate your achievements to prove that you are high functioning and not one of those other types of patients—the weepers or the navel-gazers. Plus, I used to be married to a psychologist and we socialized with other therapists, most of them very nice people, but such a window into the world of mental health professionals removed much of their mystery for me, and with it, their authority. For instance, at one gathering a woman counselor sitting across from me crossed her legs and I briefly saw her underpants. I knew it! I thought. You all wear underpants.

It wasn't many months past my Zumba meltdown that I learned that my friend Dennis, much to my surprise and delight, had decided to become an integrated life coach. Dennis notified his friends that he needed to train on real, live humans, hence he was volunteering his services if anyone wanted to be a coachee.

Me! Me! Me! I wrote back, determined to beat everyone else to this free offer. I was particularly intrigued by the idea of working with Dennis because Dennis is data driven. In fact, at his day job, Dennis is the Nostradamus of data, predicting an organization's future based on facts and statistics. He also is a deep thinker and one of the funniest people you will probably never know because what Dennis is not is a talker, let alone a pep talker. Introvert is the proper descriptor, but I would say a more apt analogy is that Dennis is like a recessed ceiling light—bright, over most of our heads, and disinclined to fully enter the room.

According to Dennis, his role as an *integrated* life coach is to help me uncover my core issues *and* develop an action plan to achieve my goals. Unlike introverted Dennis, I am a talking machine, but when it came to tapping my inner FLAWSOMEness, I liked the sound of his coaching methods—action rather than just blabbing. A plan was established, we would meet once a week for six weeks, and by the time we were done I would be a perfect person, that last part being my expectation.

Fast forward through those enlightening six weeks. It is one thing to suspect you have core issues; it is quite another thing to have them quantified and laid out for you in an elaborate narrative, replete with wings and arrows. I am referring here to the Riso-Hudson Enneagram Type Indicator, aka the Enneagram Personality Test, which Dennis had me take so that we could use the results to help me better understand what drives me. The test includes 144 paired statements, requiring you to choose between two options. When calculated, the results reveal your score for all nine Enneagram types, with your highest score determining your predominant type.

At first, the news looked good. Really good. As it turns out, I am a Type Three, The Achiever, which, not to brag, is the *star* of the nine integrated personality types, according to the folks at the Enneagram Institute. In case you are a doubter, let me reassure you that the Enneagram Institute, as the word "institute" implies, is a scientific research organization, not to be lumped in with, say Gwyneth Paltrow's Goop Lab that proffers dubious practices like vaginal steaming and "healing" stickers made from NASA spacesuits. Indeed, while the traditional Enneagram system only dates back to the 1960s, the Enneagram model of the human psyche contains components from mystical Judaism, Christianity, Islam, Taoism, Buddhism, and ancient Greek philosophy.

Since getting the scores on my Enneagram test, I have spent much time reflecting on my life as a Type Three. Threes are people (*my* people!) who want to excel and impress others. Check! We strive to be presentable and appropriate. Check! At our best, we are inner-directed, efficient, well-adjusted, charming, and organized. Hell yeah! Above all—and this was the part that resonated the most with me—Threes are goal oriented. Check plus!

For much of my time working with Dennis, he and I discussed the results of my Enneagram test, using it as a foundation for further exploration into what makes me tick. What was there to talk about? I thought at first. I was the star of the personality types, and it made perfect sense. "You're someone who gets things done," more than one friend has remarked in my past. And it was true. I have always prided myself on doing what it takes to get the job done and done right.

"Let's talk about the times when you have felt the most successful and the least successful professionally," Dennis pried, determined, alas, to do his job as an integrated life coach.

"That's easy," I said, and it was. "I feel the most successful when I have a book contract."

And so, the real work of self-awareness began. From the moment those words left my mouth I realized something both obvious and disturbing, which is how self-sabotaging this mentality is, given that 99 percent of the time I don't have a book contract, plus I would hardly hold this up as a sign of failure for other people. Indeed, as a writing instructor, I truly believe the act of writing is the most meaningful accomplishment, and for that matter I truly believe that *not* writing can be equally meaningful, depending on how you fill your time.

"I haven't written a word in months." I hear this frequently when I run into former students, as if they owe me an apology or a confession. Even odder is when someone whom I don't recognize greets me in a similar fashion.

"I feel terrible I haven't been writing," the cashier at the Quik Mart—Sharon, according to her name tag—recently admitted.

"Uh, that's okay," I said, disoriented because I had no context for this comment, and also because I was tipsy and on a late-night sugar run. What should I have said in response to this out-of-the-blue confession—"I'm sorry, too, Sharon. I feel terrible I haven't restocked the beer cave."

But now, in the light of my Enneagram results, I can see that my double standards for myself and the rest of the world might not be serving me on my journey toward FLAWSOMEness.

"You seem so busy," I remember someone commenting to me in the recent past, alluding to my workshops and a variety of other fulfilling things on my plate. "I don't know how you fit it all in."

"Really," I said, more focused on my failure to land another contract for a proposed new book project. "I don't feel like I've been doing much of anything."

Now that I am aware of the dark side of being a Three, it has become easy, actually unavoidable, to recall examples of how being a success-driven and goal-oriented Achiever has negatively impacted my behavior, my attitude, and my relationships for much of my life.

> Flashback to when my children were too young to drive. "I'll be right out," I tell them as they head to the car to await my arrival. Before I follow them, however, I feel compelled to first empty the dishwasher, balance my checkbook, scoop the kitty litter, swab on mascara, switch the laundry from the washer to the dryer . . . Who wants to come home to all those tasks? But

then my kids grew up, and now they have trust issues, at least when it comes to letting me drive.

I am under deadline and laser-focused. "Do you need anything from the grocery store?" The asker might be my ex-husband or Helmut—it really doesn't matter because while my mates have changed, my response remains the same. I make a point to linger on the task in front of me, like one of those CEOs who purposely waits to look up from his all-important papers when an underling enters his corner office. I read once that one in five CEOs is a psychopath and, while contrary to popular belief not every psychopath is a murderer, they are, as one psychologist put it, just people with really odious personalities.

"Don't get mad," Helmut recently said to me, after he surprised me with a new washing machine. My gosh, a new washing machine! How could I possibly be mad? Then he reminded me of my recent fit when I tried to reconstruct one of those flat mailers with a thousand perforations and slotted tabs. Given that performance and countless others like it, he was simply trying to preempt my hissy fit when I tried to figure out how to adjust this new machine's spin cycle.

There is a saying: be careful what you wish for, you may just get it. At first, I felt relief to have my personality quantified to a Three, the star of the personality types. But now I have mixed feelings, similar to those I imagine experienced by a long-suffering patient who finally receives a proper diagnosis. "The tests are conclusive," I envision an earnest young doctor delivering this news, her face a mask of compassion and steady eye contact, the result of a medical school education that clearly included an elective on empathy. "You suffer from a task deficiency," she explains. "In layperson's terms that means that when you are working on a goal, you experience a spike in your drive-to-succeed levels. But when you fail at that goal, or when you are struggling to learn something new, you feel like a pathetic loser."

Months have passed since the completion of my six coaching sessions with Dennis, but in the aftermath, I have had to seriously confront the dark side of being a Three, mostly because it manifests almost every single day. What happens when a Three is out of whack?

• We only feel valued for our accomplishments.

• We measure our own self-worth and success on tasks achieved and goals met.

• When focused on a job, we brush aside other people's feelings or needs.

• We pretend everything is fine even when it is not.

Check, check, hell yeah, and check. In the years before my personality was quantified by Dennis and the Enneagram folks, I was comfortable with my lack of insight, or rather I was better able to disguise my failings as *bogus* failings, a clever trick to project an image of success, the way a person applying for a job might respond when an interviewer asks, "Tell me something you feel you need to work on."

"Oh, I guess I care too much about doing a good job."

Puhleeze. While I have never said something that ridiculous at a job interview, my Enneagram results have made it clear: I have spent a lifetime trying to bury my failings and feelings in a false construct. But now I knew, being a Three was much to blame for my past discontent and did not bode well for my future, unless I was willing to learn (ugh) how to change.

There is no right or wrong when it comes to Zumba, I tell myself as I maneuver once again for a place in the back of the class. I am back among the kettlebells, and this time I am determined to let loose and have fun. In addition, this time I am not going to allow any latecomer to elbow me out of my rightful place. The instructor is the same woman whose hot pink tank top was much of the inspiration for me seeking help when help (in the form of the Nostradamus of data) presented itself.

FLAWSOME. I think about the word as I struggle to synchronize my arms with my feet. In the context of the Enneagram personality test, it sounds like something a Four (the Enthusiast) would say, with their fun-loving, busy, and versatile but scattered minds. As a writer, I appreciate the clever wordplay. We can be awesome even with our flaws. We can stink at Zumba and still have a good time.

The instructor slaps her thigh and starts swiveling in one direction, while the rest of us pivot randomly like Rock 'Em, Sock 'Em Robots. There is no right or wrong in Zumba, I remind myself, trying to offset my growing frustration. But there is, I think, otherwise what is the point?

"Did you have fun?" the instructor asks me after class. In response I give her two thumbs up, while imagining myself kicking her shins. Before, I would have blamed my feelings of failure on the fact that this instructor is lousy at instructing, or on all the athleisure blocking my view. But now that I am further along on my journey toward self-awareness, I know that my real problem is that I am a Three. I am an Achiever who is not achieving 99 percent of the time. I am a writer, albeit one often without a book contract, but if there is one thing this writer does not need to learn, it is that FLAWSOME is an oxymoron.

Hot as Hell

There are two things I love about the little Church of Christ I pass on my occasional jogs down Route 14. One is that the church people opted for an unusual lime-green paint for the parish house. The other is the messages they post on the church's street-facing sign, which almost always give me a boost. Sometimes the messages are simply announcements of their ham-and-beans community dinners, but other times they offer witty commentary (*No, it's not hot as hell.*) or inspirational missives (*Feeling down? Look up!*). When I'm particularly tired on a run, I'll imagine myself in a marathon, with the Lord himself holding up the church sign as he cheers me on from the sidelines. A couple months ago, however, the church posted a message that still has me thinking: *Only you can end racism.*

I'm not going to lie. My first thought after reading that message was, Why do I have to do everything? For one thing, I'm not a racist, at least if you don't count all the ways I benefit from white privilege. I know I—and my "extra light with cool undertones" skin tone (according to Sephora cosmetics)—can walk into any boutique, and no security personnel are going to make a point to monitor my movements, which is not only unfair to people of color, but also ironic, given that I used to be quite the shoplifter back in my twenties. Even now, when I see those stacks of individually wrapped toilet paper rolls in public restrooms, the impulse returns. "Don't do it," I whisper to myself, while thinking, *But isn't that why you carry such a bulky shoulder bag?*

I also know that if I find myself driving slowly through a rich neighborhood, rap music booming from my car speakers, people are going to assume the truth—which is that I am horribly lost rather than casing the fancy houses, and that I got a little rambunctious on my Pandora shuffle play. Similarly, in school I never experienced unfair punishment or grading policies because of my skin color; I have never been denied a bank loan for no good reason; I have never been profiled at airports or traffic stops; and I have never faced job discrimination because of the way I wear my hair, even back in the nineties, when prejudice against my perm would have actually been justified. In short, all that white privilege and more I can own up to, but it still doesn't explain why—according to the good people of the Church of Christ—it's all on me to end racism.

Of course the message on the church sign was simply a figure of speech, not meant to be taken literally. The message is also a clear riff on the Smokey the Bear slogan, "Only YOU can prevent wildfires!" an ad campaign the U.S. Forest Service has been using in some iteration for over seventy years. Indeed, that campaign was so popular that Smokey the Bear's name and image are protected by the Smokey Bear Act of 1952, and even now, according to the ad council, eight in ten outdoor recreationists recognize the icon.

For some reason, I don't feel the same pressure or defensiveness when Smokey the Bear tells me that I am the only one who can prevent wildfires. Reading the Forest Service's message, I've never felt accused, like Smokey is assuming I'm out there negligently flicking my butts onto dry oak leaves or leaving my campfire wieners unattended. Maybe because this directive is coming from a fur-covered cartoon sporting a broad-brimmed hat and jeans, I'm less threatened by his figure of speech. Plus, every time I see that message, even while I should be thinking about the devastation caused by wildfires, I find myself distracted. Is his real name Smokey the Bear, I wonder, or Smokey Bear? And if it's the first version, isn't his species pretty obvious?

Only I can end racism? At last count, there were 7.8 billion people in the world. Thus, technically speaking, I should be expected to carry only 1/7.8 billionth of a percent of the responsibility for this enormous and intractable problem. I do fully acknowledge that it's not simply on the targets of racism to do something about the issue, any more than sexual harassment is a woman's problem. Addressing bigotry and hate crimes against minorities or groups outside our own identity are never just the victims' burden. But how much can one white woman do to end racism? How much should one white woman do?

I think about an encounter I had a few years ago when I crashed a birthday celebration for my friend's Grandma Nanette, who was turning ninety-four. (My friend assured me the more the merrier at this family gathering, so off I went for a little road trip to the assisted living facility.) The nonagenarian birthday girl was so smiley, so happy to share her ribbon candy, so prone to warm hugs, even with party crashers like me whom she had never met, that I quickly understood why even outsiders call her Grandma Nanette.

But, as it turned out, Grandma Nanette was also a bit of a racist. (Or is racist like pregnant, you either are or you aren't?) To her credit, Grandma Nanette wasn't the N-word-spewing kind of racist, but don't get her started on Prince Harry's marriage to Meghan Markle. "But what if their child is dark-skinned?" she asked me, when our brief conversation (prompted by a *People* magazine resting on the side table) turned to Meghan's pregnancy, a focus of celebrity news at the time. "The royal family has to be concerned."

I was taken aback to hear such an ugly remark coming from such a nice old woman at her birthday party. On the ride over to the little celebration, my friend had offered some stories about Grandma Nanette. How she had married the love of her life, Bob, when she was just a teenager, before he left to fight Hitler. After the war, the couple had settled in Maine where he learned the pharmacy trade, and she worked at the phone company until the children came along. For years, Grandma Nanette had volunteered so many hours at the hospital auxiliary that the medical center's gift shop is dedicated in her name (presumably her full name, not just "Grandma Nanette"). But my friend had never mentioned that Grandma Nanette didn't approve of dark-skinned babies, at least not in the British royal family.

The church sign resurrected a question I've had since my one and only conversation with Grandma Nanette. Should I have called her out for her racist comment? Should I have tried to start a dialogue with her, engage in a meaningful way, "lean in" to the discomfort, in the hopes of authentic and productive conversation? Should I have done any or all of those things, rather than what I did do, which was say something like, "Uh, I didn't think anyone made ribbon candy anymore?"

It seems that, if I am the only one who can end racism, this reality would allow for no time off, no exceptions, no rationalizing when confronted with the Grandma Nanettes of the world. With this burden solely on my shoulders, there would be no room for thoughts like—Let it go. Don't bother arguing. She'll be dead soon enough. (Is this even a strategy—to simply wait for racists to die?)

On the other hand, if exceptions to my anti-racism efforts were allowed, wouldn't confronting Grandma Nanette be among them? After all, I was an interloper at her birthday party. On top of that, she is one of the few women still alive from the Greatest Generation. If it wasn't for her soldier husband and people like him, I probably wouldn't even exist, given my own Grandma Mae was Jewish and lived in Europe during dangerous times. So perhaps it would be okay to let Grandma Nanette enjoy her birthday party in peace, but what I could do is take on her 1/7.8th billion share of the responsibility for racism, which, in effect, would double my own.

But would this be enough? Are any of my efforts enough? I have educated myself on the signs of casual racism and how they can manifest in microaggressions. I own up to my white fragility and try my hardest not to be squirmy when the conversation turns to race. I don't go around asking to touch Black people's hair. I don't equate American with white. I don't go around saying things like, "I don't see color" or "All lives matter." I don't ask minorities what I can do to help because I know it is not on them to tell me how to overcome racism. I would never ask a Black mother of a mixed-race baby if that were her child. I understand why calling an Asian woman "cute" is not a welcome compliment. (I do think Asian babies are preternaturally cute, but I am only human.)

But are these efforts enough?

Of course not. Nothing feels like enough. And yet it all feels like too much.

I know, I know. Who am I to grumble at the relentlessness of trying to end racism when the victims of racism don't exactly get a break. It's not like nonwhite people can wake up one Tuesday and think, I just can't deal with any of this nonsense. I'm going to fetch that white-person skin out of the dirty laundry so I don't have to put up with any racist crap today.

But sometimes I don't know how much I can take on; how not to feel inadequate, or guilty, or defensive. Only I can end racism. Only I can prevent forest fires. In my sense of overwhelm it's easy for these issues to get conflated into one big maelstrom, with Smokey the Bear pointing his fat, furry paw at me, insisting that I not only take it upon myself to smother every spark within 193 million acres of national forests and grasslands, but also to prevent all the prejudice, discrimination, and hate against minorities. Heck, while I'm at it, why don't I also solve the climate crisis, and world hunger, and rescue all those endangered species?

Yesterday, I decided to run down Route 14 again and noticed the Church of Christ was still posting the same message—"Only you can end racism"—even though it had already been up for over a month. *Only you can end racism. Only you can end racism. Only you can end racism.* The refrain repeated in my head, keeping time with my footfalls. I know the church people are dealing with a limited amount of space on their sign, so they need to keep their messaging pithy. On the other hand, I would argue, we're talking about a problem—racism—that is built into the structural foundation of, well, almost everything in America—our history, our legal system, housing, education, and on and on. So isn't boiling down the solution to five words nothing more than guilt-inducing oversimplification? But—on the other hand again—where else does change start, if not with personal responsibility?

Just replace the damn message and leave me in peace, I thought, as I jogged past the church's lime-green parish house. Why couldn't this do-gooder congregation just stick to announcing its ham-and-beans suppers, or posting one of its inspirational or witty quotes. I used to like imagining the Lord holding up this church sign, cheering me on from the sidelines, but now it felt like he was pointing a finger. "It's all on you, sister," I imagined God's booming voice following me down Route 14. "You think you can just run through life not touching Black people's hair and that's going to be enough? Why should you get off so easy when there's so much work to be done? Oh, and by the way," I could just hear God adding with a sly wink, "I *purposely* made Asian babies cuter than white babies, but you didn't hear that from me."

And so it came to pass. Clearly, the Lord had spoken unto me via a little church sign, and his message was obvious. There would be no breather, no break in this endless marathon of trying to outrun my white privilege. No, it's not hot as hell, I recalled one of the previous messages on the sign, back when all I had to worry about were the inconveniences of eternal damnation. But it can sure feel like it, I thought, now that it's all on me to prevent those fires.

The Grandpa Robe

"I need a bathrobe."

This had been my winter refrain for years, but finally I decided to do something about it. Despite flannel pajamas, thick, pilled sweaters, and a well-insulated condo, I often felt chilly in my house. I know some people (our friend Nick, for example) who keep their homes at fifty-five degrees when they are at work during the day, then light the woodstove when they return home. I, however, as a middle-aged creature of comfort, do not have that kind of time or blood flow.

"Is anyone else freezing?" Many times, people in my domestic sphere of influence—which includes Helmut, my two daughters, and even my ex-husband—have offered to buy me a bathrobe, if only to stop hearing me repeat that question while cranking up the thermostat to temperatures on par with Finland's World Sauna Championships. But as much as I love gifts, I could not accept their largesse. Despite the fact that, typically, I have zero standards when it comes to loungewear, I knew that my bathrobe—when I found it—had to be just right for me:

No satin or silk, such chilly fabrics, like something the matriarch in a sexless marriage would wear on an evening soap opera

A substantive weight but not heavy; the length neither

floor-sweeping (too British dressing gown) nor skimpy (too *Real Housewives of Beverly Hills*)

Definitely no scotch plaid (too androcratic)

No fleece (too staticky)

My friend Nawal (wife of the aforementioned Nick) works at a fancy store that sells luxury textiles. Based on her recommendation, I checked out the robes at her shop and wow! I rubbed my cheek against a spa-style waffle weave of 100 percent linen-cotton, which is apparently stiffer than regular cotton so that the robe serves not only as a robe, but also as an invigorating exfoliant! Even if this spa-worthy robe had not been out of my price range, it felt too swanky for me, though I could imagine the more stylish Nawal swathed in one. Or, more likely, swathed in four, while she shivered and waited for Nick to fire up the woodstove after their return home from work.

Then, one day in early December, I found it. I found the perfect bathrobe.

"What's so special about this robe?" Helmut asked, after I modeled it for him in our kitchen. You would think the way it transformed me into a plus-size pupa would have made the answer obvious.

"It spoke to me," I answered, which was not far from the truth. I had been online, browsing the L.L. Bean website where I have shopped countless times before, though mostly for the men in my life. That day, however, as I sat and scrolled in my living room, I could tell I was getting warm, warmer, cozy, cozier, and then—there it was, a calf-length cotton French terry cloth robe with a tie belt and roomy front pockets. Machine wash and dry. Imported. (Really, L.L. Bean? *Imported*?) Whatever. I preferred the light-blue option but something, some whisper inside my head, told me to choose vintage indigo.

The first time I donned my new robe there was one thing I knew for sure—it would be hard to ever take it off.

"Is it warm enough?" Helmut asked me that night as we were reading next to each other on the couch. I gave his hand a squeeze, meaning yes. The gesture is part of an unspoken language I created, as a way to respond when I feel too tired or disinclined to talk. One squeeze means "yes." Two means "no." A tap means "I love you," and so on. I explained to Helmut my rationale for this silent form of communication: "It will come in handy," I told him, "when one of us can no longer talk."

Sadly, I did have to take off the robe and put on normal-people clothes whenever I left the house to travel beyond the mailbox, but usually I put it back on almost as soon as I arrived home. I quickly became so attached to my robe that it brought to mind that fairy tale about the spoiled girl who can't resist wearing her new red shoes all the time, even to church. But then a mysterious old soldier curses the red shoes so they are impossible to remove, forcing the girl to keep dancing, dancing, dancing . . . I felt like my robe was starting to have the same sway over me, though instead of dancing, dancing, dancing I couldn't stop lounging, lounging, lounging.

"It's my grandpa robe," I announced one day, when I caught sight of my bulky silhouette reflected in our full-length mirror. At the time, I thought I was simply making a generic observation, based on the way I looked and felt as I puttered around the house. As it turned out, however, this was indeed my grandpa robe, but in ways more significant than I had yet to discover.

It is a Sunday mid-afternoon, and I am making myself a lox and bagel sandwich, still in my grandpa robe, despite the hour. This is one of my favorite meals and has been since my early childhood spent among Jewish relatives on my dad's side. Here is the thing about a lox and bagel sandwich. It is one of my favorite sandwiches *only* if prepared to my exact specifications: One half of a toasted everything bagel, buttered, with a thick layer of cream cheese. Two slivers of lox. Plus onions and capers.

Finally! My perfectly constructed sandwich is ready to eat.

"You forgot the tomato! How can you eat a lox and bagel sandwich without the tomato?"

What? The voice is so clear, so recognizable that I glance around my kitchen.

"Daddy?" For most of my childhood and well beyond, my dad and

I enjoyed an ongoing debate—how to make the perfect lox and bagel sandwich. I had my version, while my dad's was to pile on the tomato and go light on the onion. Plus, he topped his sandwich with a bagel lid.

"The tomato makes it too squishy," I would argue. "And there's way too much bagel if you use both halves."

Until now, I had forgotten all about this little back-and-forth between me and my dad. In truth, I had forgotten the sound of his voice, and so many other things about him. My dad has been dead for well over a decade, due in large part to a stroke that took his life, though it didn't actually kill him for another six years.

"What were your parents like?" Helmut, whom I met several years after both my parents were gone, has asked me this question on several occasions. I tell him I had a happy childhood. I know that I loved my mom and dad. I know that they took good care of me and continued to do so long into my adulthood. But whenever I tried recalling specific memories, the few that surfaced were always from those last, miserable years, as if the trauma of my father's long decline, swiftly followed by my mother's enfeeblement, overwrote all the positive memories in my hippocampus.

Yet now, in the kitchen of my condo as I eat my perfectly constructed lox-and-bagel sandwich, it feels like my dad—my dad before his stroke—is right here with me, piling on the tomato and topping it off with a bagel lid.

A few days later, I am writing at my desk, as usual wearing my grandpa robe, when I have a similar experience.

"We're going for a quick trip to the grocery store. Why don't you keep us company?" My dad is holding a leash attached to our Saint Bernard. "We won't be gone long," he pats Alice, who is grinning, a string of saliva dangling from her jowls. Alice is always grinning when she is with my dad.

"Just the grocery store," I insist, "nowhere else!" (In this memory, the "I" is me around age twelve.) My dad was notorious for promising a quick errand run and then holding me or his entire family hostage in the backseat of our Buick LeSabre while he and Alice made one boring stop after another, the longest delay usually at the hardware store.

"Come on," he coaxes as the scene plays out in my mind. "Alice is driving."

Not that old joke again, I think, and can't help but smile. I remember how it always made me roll my eyes. But of course, I rode along on those errand runs anyway because I liked hanging out with my dad, and somewhere between his endless conversations about hinges and sprockets, I knew that he would treat us to dusty-road sundaes.

"Are your parents still alive?" I still get this question from time to time, mostly from people around my age who are caring for their own elderly parents. They talk about their mom's latest fall or wonder aloud if they should take away their dad's car keys. Sometimes they talk about the love they have for their parents, but mostly I hear about the stress of dealing with chronic health crises and waiting for the inevitable end.

Relief. I still feel awful admitting this, but since my dad died, I have felt nothing but relief that those last years of his life are behind us.

It happens again, in the quiet of an early morning. I am wrapped in my grandpa robe, sitting alone in my living room, my mind drifting. Then, I am neither alone nor at home. I am in my parents' family room in the house where I grew up, back for a visit with my daughters, just little girls in this memory. My dad is on his hands and knees on the braided rug, playing horsey with them.

"Don't get them all worked up," my mom says. She is sitting in her usual spot on the couch, already on her third cup of coffee and third load of wash. I know, of course, it is not my little girls she wishes to remain calm but rather my dad who had a heart attack a few years earlier. But in the time of this memory my dad is feeling dandy. He is nearing seventy, retired from his job as an engineer of farm equipment, and loving his life of leisure and travel and solving the world's problems with his buddies.

Equally notable in this scene, my parents' family room has been restored to how it used to be before the rug was removed to accommodate my dad's wheelchair during those anxiety-ridden occasions when we tried to bring him back to his house for visits after his stroke. Until now, my memory of this room has been overrun with boxes of latex gloves and packages of Depends. Yet now, like a miracle, this family room is restored to a happier time I had all but forgotten.

"My turn, Grandpa! My turn!" my daughters clamor.

They can't get enough of this man who adored them, though the years afforded them to really appreciate their grandpa were cut way too short by his stroke.

Grandpa.

The happy scene vaporizes in a flash of comprehension. Now I understand. I have so named my beloved robe the "grandpa robe" not just because of the way I putter around in it like an old person, but because this is an exact replica of the robe that belonged to my dad in his later, sick years, after he was as much a grandpa as my father. Like the one that swaddles me now, my dad's robe was also from L.L. Bean, terry cloth and calf-length, with a tie belt and roomy front pockets. The color: vintage indigo.

What compelled me to choose this identical robe—if anything a symbol of my father's diminishment—speaks to the mysteries of the mind in the aftermath of trauma. Here, I am not referring to the trauma suffered by my father, but to my own trauma, in which a lifetime of good memories of my dad got lost in the wake of that one massive cerebrovascular shitstorm.

Just pull the plug. Just pull the plug. It happens again on one of the chilliest nights of the winter. I am in bed, wearing my grandpa robe over my pajamas. A scene from the past plays out in my mind: My dad is in the hospital, being kept alive by a ventilator, while I sit beside him holding his hand. *Just pull the plug. Just pull the plug.*

I shake my head and sit up in my own bed to disperse this awful memory. My grandpa robe has betrayed me. It was supposed to be the perfect robe for me—comforting and substantive, but not too heavy. I had come to see this robe as almost magical, the one thing that could not only ward off my perpetual chill but serve as a portal to a past full of positive memories. But this remembrance—sitting at my father's deathbed—is absolutely the worst.

"I'm sorry," I say, either in my head or aloud. Time conflates, and while I know it has been years since I last saw my father alive, it feels like

I am back with him at his bedside, holding the bones of his hand. "I'm sorry for wanting to pull the plug. I'm sorry for wanting you to die." My dad is gone, and yet he is here.

"Can you forgive me?" I ask him, but that was never the question. What I am really asking is this—Is it okay to forgive myself for wishing an end to his life? In the dark chill of the bedroom, I can feel my dad give my hand a squeeze, as perceptible as the comfort provided me by my grandpa robe. My dad's breathing tube prevents him from speaking, but I know how to interpret his answer. In my unspoken language, his single squeeze is as good as a yes.

Dear Ex (Ex?) Friend

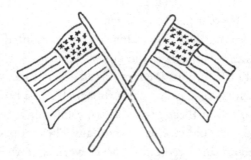

Dear Ex (Ex?) Friend,

I hadn't seen you for a couple years, not since politics cleaved our friendship. Then all of the sudden there you were on this early winter morning, crossing my path in the gym parking lot. And before I could remember that you are a Republican and I am the opposite; before I could remember my vow to never, ever forgive Trump supporters—including you—you hugged me hello. And I hugged you back.

The relief, to feel love instead of anger.

"How's the writing going?" you asked.

"Did you ever apply for that new job?" I followed up.

"Can you believe this weather? When's the last time we had this much snow?"

We lingered in the parking lot as the sun rose higher in the sky, cutting the chill. Our exchange was just small talk—not like all those heart-to-hearts, and laugh fests, and shared secrets that had once brought us close and kept us sane and made life a lot more fun, even when it wasn't. Still, given the distance between us these past years, even small talk felt like a big deal.

For what seems like forever, I have tried to not feel such . . . betrayal. I have lectured myself so many times. *Try to understand her point of view. Forget about our political differences. What could be more important than friendship?* But always, I hit a wall. *Who would help put a racist in the White House, but another racist? Who would still support a man who bragged about grabbing women by the pussy, labeled Mexicans rapists, mocked disabled reporters, put children in cages, and denied an entire election?*

You! I thought, with that goddamn elephant T-shirt in your closet that you loved to wear just to goad me.

This morning in the parking lot, you pointed to your feet. "Remember these," you raised the cuff of your jeans, displaying socks of red wool, shot with blue. We reminisced about a party Helmut and I had hosted years ago—a different world ago. He had brought out a big, cardboard box full of these luxury socks, each pair hand-knit over the years by his 101-year-old mother in Germany. They represented decades-worth of love and fine needlework, never worn, soft, rich in color. (But really, how many socks can one son wear?) At the gathering, you and our other friends all selected a pair or two to take home. A lovely way to spread the warmth.

"I think of you guys every time I wear these socks," you said. "One foot is you, and the other is Helmie." (I remember when you assigned him that pet name, after you'd finally deigned him worthy of my affections.)

I laughed, imagining Helmut and I as sock puppets on your feet. By now, the gym parking lot was half full and the sun was shining in my eyes, blinding me, so I shifted position. You were such a good friend, I thought with a pang. One hug in a parking lot had brought it all back. Then you were my ex-friend, but what happens now? If we were to let it all go, the politics, the angry rhetoric, the polarity of our views, would we become ex ex-friends? Would that allow us to get back to where we had started?

In the parking lot, we said goodbye with vague promises to get together. You headed to your SUV, and I got into my hybrid. As I waited for my car to warm up, I thought about you showing off your socks, and a lame joke popped into my head—"You know," I could have said, "those are both *left* socks you're wearing on your feet."

Too soon, I thought, but at least it kindled the hint of a smile.

Clearing the Air

Not for the first time I was complaining about a woman who used to participate repeatedly in my writing workshops. "She always has to be the center of attention," I said to my friend Frances as we were strolling down a tree-lined path near my house. "Other people in class will be reading their work aloud for feedback and she'll be clacking away on her laptop, not even pretending to pay attention. Clack. Clack. Clack!"

Ever since this woman—let's call her Luna—came into my life, insisting she would be lost without my writing guidance, she has rubbed me the wrong way, so much so that I had fantasized about banning her from my classes, that is until she dropped out a couple years ago. No heads up. No explanation. Good riddance, I thought at the time, but also, how rude!

"You know she calls herself 'The Medium Maven,'" I continued my tirade, "which doesn't even make sense if you really think about it. Plus, every time she starts bragging about her so-called psychic powers, it reminds me of that kid's taunt: *I know something you don't know . . .*"

What prompted this screed was Frances telling me about one of her own experiences with a medium back in 2020. Frances ascribes to all things New Age, but for once even she had her doubts. The medium had asked her if she knew someone whose first name began with K. Apparently, this dead K person wanted Frances to know that she could expect something of great value to come her way in March, though it wouldn't be in the form of money.

Let's see, I thought, what happened in March 2020? That's right, a pandemic.

"I can't think of anyone I know who has passed whose name starts with K," my perplexed friend had admitted.

"What is it with mediums and initials?" I posed the question that has long flummoxed me. "If psychics really can communicate with the dead, why don't they just ask the person for their full name?" Without waiting for an answer, I continued to rattle on about my issues with Luna.

"So then," I told Frances, "after Luna stopped taking my workshops, and I thought I was finally rid of her, I get this email with the subhead: "The energy moves and you feel better." Can you believe it!? Luna had subscribed me to her Medium Maven newsletter hawking her full moon clearings! And there's no way to unsubscribe! Believe me, I've tried." I kicked a stone on the path. "What. A. Bitch."

"You know," Frances interjected, "Luna died last weekend."

"What?" I stopped dead in my tracks, no pun intended.

"That woman you're talking about, Luna, she died a couple days ago. I heard it from some people in her church."

"How?" I asked.

"I think she had liver cancer," my friend said. "Apparently, she went downhill really fast."

"I'll say," I responded in a state of disbelief. One minute I was bitching about the woman, and the next minute she was dead.

I know firsthand how hard it is when people you love die, but after the news of Luna's death I realized it is a different kind of hard when someone you vehemently dislike dies. I know I should feel terrible. My God, the woman suffered from liver cancer, or something equally cruel and rapacious. She must have been terrified when she heard her prognosis. At least I would have been terrified. Plus, Luna and I were close in age, which in my fervent opinion means that she was way too young to die.

I also know that, despite my animosity toward her, Luna was not a bad person. In fact, as hard as it was for me to fathom, people seemed to value her work and enjoy her company. I saw someone who sucked all the air out of the room, whereas many others saw a colorful character with a sharp wit. I saw a charlatan, but they saw a healer. One day after class I overheard a workshop participant who also happened to be one of Luna's clients thanking her for unblocking her sacral chakra. "It's like the sky is bluer," the woman had told her.

As if.

Even after she died, Luna still managed to provoke my anger, usually stoked by any mention of mediums, energy work, the full moon, and of course the arrival of her blasted monthly newsletter, which seemed to appear weekly in my inbox. I am enlightened enough to know that if someone ignites negative feelings in you to a disproportionate degree, it probably says more about you than them. But what? It was not as if I disliked all people with New Age beliefs, thank goodness, otherwise I would not like half of my closest friends. Yet, in the weeks since her death, Luna seemed to be bugging me more than usual. I would be on a hike, or dicing a poblano pepper, or procrastinating at my writing desk and find myself getting all worked up. I even created fantasies in my overactive imagination. A recent example:

I am teaching a workshop in heaven and Luna is one of the participants. Our small group is gathered in a circle, sitting on comfy clouds, so much nicer than the mismatched furniture in my earthly writer's center in White River Junction, Vermont. The writers introduce themselves.

"Hi, I'm T. It seems I never had time to start that novel when I was alive . . ."

"Hi, I'm S, and I'm working on a memoir . . ."

"Darlings, I'm the Medium Maven, but you can call me L . . ."

Ugh, I think, wrenching myself out of this fantasy. Luna's vocal fry is no less grating in the afterlife.

About a month after Luna's passing, I am working at my desk when an email pops into my inbox. *The energy moves and you feel better.*

"UNSUBSCRIBE ME YOU MOTHERFUCKER!"

Then I remember that Luna is dead. But what if . . . I hesitate to finish my next thought. What if she is trying to reach me from beyond the veil? She was a medium, after all, or so she claimed. *Someone whose first name starts with L wants to tell you something.* My curious finger can't help but click open the email.

"Dear friend of our mother . . ." The message, as it turns out, is not from Luna but rather from her son and daughter, both young adults, thanking me for subscribing to their mom's newsletter. "My kids are amazing," Luna had frequently bragged in our workshops, apropos of absolutely nothing to do with narrative craft. "Their father was a dick, but the kids are perfect." Oh how Luna loved causing ripples with this type of ballsy pronouncement.

The email is also an invitation to an online sale her children have put together to disperse Luna's spiritual paraphernalia: healing crystals, chakra pendulums, essential oils, pendants, her library of astrology books and tarot cards. This must have been a brutal task for Luna's kids, sorting through the artifacts of their mother's trade. I can just imagine my own daughters peddling the earthly belongings that served my life as a writer. *Dear friend of our mother, check out the following now on sale: a bunch of lightly used journals, a coffee mug with a photo of our mom's cat, and one of those happy lamps to cheer you up when you're sun deprived or feeling sluggish. Our mom used hers as a desk lamp!*

Because I feel sorry for Luna's kids (and my own), I go to her website, but instead of trawling through Luna's New Age estate sale, I click on a video of her talking about her work.

"Each energy clearing is truly life changing," Luna starts her spiel. She is dressed all in white, which (note to self) packs on at least five extra pounds. "It's fascinating to see people transform," she continues, "to see how they can just let go, and even laugh at their negative patterns . . ." I make myself watch to the end, on the off chance that something truly psychic might occur, say, Luna addresses me by name, or her ectoplasm starts oozing from my monitor. After that does not happen, I head outside for a walk.

It is a sunny fall afternoon, and I stroll down the very same tree-lined path where I first learned of Luna's passing from Frances. A memory pops into my head. It is the last time I saw Luna, about a year after she had dropped out of my workshop. We were both at an open mic night for writers. Most of the performers read poems aloud, but Luna shared a short story, a piece I remember she had been working on in class.

"Was it any good?" Luna asked me when she passed my table after her performance.

"You did great," I said. "The writing was fantastic." When it comes to offering positive feedback, this is the one area where I am my own better angel. When I like a writer's work—even if I do not like the person—I feel compelled to tell them, lest I become one of those emotionally constipated people painfully backed up with positive feedback and compliments they refuse to give others out of spite, or pettiness, or jealousy.

"So, you really thought my story was good?" Luna persisted. "I didn't make a fool of myself?" I felt a flare of annoyance, recalling all too well Luna's habit of fishing for compliments.

"The audience loved it," I reassured her.

She started to walk away then turned back to me. "I should take another one of your of workshops," she said. "If for nothing else, I could use the deadlines."

Shit! Too late, I realized my terrible mistake. Shit! Shit! Shit! I was as stupid as those people who invite vampires inside their home, which, according to lore, is the only way they can enter your house. I feared my appreciation of Luna's writing would be all the invitation she needed to return to my workshops and suck the lifeblood right out of them.

Around the next curve of the tree-lined path, a bench presents itself, and I stretch out my legs. In the aftermath of that last encounter with Luna, I had expected to hear from her every time I advertised a new round of classes. Knowing me, I never would have had the gumption to turn her away. You cannot just encourage someone at a reading and then exclude that person from your class simply because you find her obnoxious. Or at least I cannot do such a thing, not without expecting some kind of cosmic comeuppance. And so, I would have to endure her participation until she quit again on her own; either that or until one of us died.

"And now one of us has died." Luna's vocal fry comes out of nowhere. I look around but the path is empty. "So maybe," she continues, "you should just let it go." In my mind's eye she gives me one of her trademark I-know-something-you-don't-know winks.

Let it go. On her promotional video Luna had talked about how she helps her clients do just that, thanks to her energy clearings.

Let it go, my ass, I think. Or rather, that is what I usually think when someone like Luna offers me this type of advice. Let it go? But rights must be wronged! People must pay! I am entitled to all my anger! But this afternoon I am of a different mindset. Maybe it is because I am outside on this beautiful autumn day. Or maybe it is the memory of Luna dressed all in white, telling me that one day I will look back on my negative patterns and laugh.

And I do find myself smiling, not at Luna's premature passing, but at her ballsy pronouncements and sneaky psychic powers. Luna is dead—the reality hits me in a way that I had previously failed to fully comprehend. One of us has indeed died, as she has just reminded me only minutes ago, which means that I will never have to suffer her clack, clack, clacking in any more of my workshops.

I take a long draught of the refreshing air and tilt my face up to the sun. My relief is palpable, physical, as if something heavy has been dislodged from my being. My energy has moved, I realize, and, wonder of wonders, I actually do feel lighter, better, just as Luna had predicted. It really is like the sky is bluer. I can see this now with my very own eyes and—credit where credit is due—I owe it all to Luna, the Medium Maven whom I never liked in life, but know enough not to doubt in death.

May both she, and I, finally rest in peace.

No Podium for Old Men
A Transcript of the Introductory Remarks at the "Diversity Enhancement Award" Ceremony at Walter S. Walters College

Welcome ladies and gentlemen.

Tonight, it is my special privilege to introduce this evening's honoree and speaker. She is the youngest faculty member at Walter S. Walters College to receive the "Distinguished Master Teacher Prize," er, I mean the recently renamed "Diversity Enhancement Award." Last semester she was listed in a student poll as—let me find my other pair of glasses to make sure I am reading this correctly—"the coolest professor to rock lit." And, on a personal note, as someone who has served as both department chair and interim dean (1971 to '79) at this fine institution, and who has devoted the entirety of his scholarship to the Western canon, I hold tonight's honoree and speaker singularly responsible for the name change from "English Department" to "Department of Literatures."

So, without further ado or ad absurdum, please join me in welcoming . . .

[Voices from the audience: "We can't hear you." "Turn on the microphone."]

What? Oh dear. Can you hear me now? Is this thing on? Damn modern technology.

[Chair scraping. Indistinguishable muttering.]

Well now, let us resume, but first, a small round of applause for our aspiring graduate Mr. Jesse Pepperidge and his assistance just now with the audio equipment. May his talents one day extend to a deeper understanding of the main themes of *Coriolanus*. Mr. Pepperidge, let me remind you that I am expecting the fifth draft of your thesis on my desk next Friday at four.

Now where was I? Ah yes. Tradition. When I was a young buck new to these hallowed halls, my feelings of humility were second only to my sense of awe. How could I, a minister's son from Ohio, fresh from my doctoral defense, be worthy to teach in the prestigious Walter S. Walters English Department, er, the Department of Literatures. Yet, it was the chair of the department himself, Doctor Otto O. Kendricks—the leading scholar on the Universalism of Esotericism—who offered me the position and took me under his wing.

"You are home." Those were the exact words of welcome proffered by Doctor Kendricks on my first day, as he stood behind this very podium at which I now stand. And home is what Walter S. Walters College has been to me for these past sixty years. Somehow, my schoolboy dream of being a professor of literature at a renowned institution was made manifest, and to this day I remain grateful. Yet, as William Butler Yeats once wrote, "In dreams begin responsibilities." And since I have evoked the spirit of Yeats, would any student in attendance care to tell me from which poem that line is taken?

Mr. Yang?

Miss Smythe?

You can stop waving at me, Ms. Cole, we all know you know the answer.

Mr. Pepperidge? Your hand is raised? I daresay, my physician would disapprove of such a shock to my weakened heart. But please, share with us your knowledge of the poem I was just quoting?

[Voice from the audience: "Professor, I was wondering if you could stop calling me Mister Pepperidge? I identify as non-binary and prefer they/them."]

Oh dear. [sigh] I admit to a befuddlement around the concept of *they* as a singular third-person pronoun. Still, one can argue neither with the inevitability of semantic change, nor the wisdom of William Shakespeare: *This above all: to thine own self be true.* Therefore, you have my word Mister, er, Mister They? Mister Them? Oh dear. Jesse, if you would please do me the honor of coming to see me during office hours so that I can further enlighten you on *Coriolanus*, and you can further enlighten me on the proper pronoun best suited to your identity.

Now where was I? Ah yes. Responsibilities. I took mine seriously as an educator, a molder of young minds, an ambassador to truth, virtue, and the sacred through the prose and poetry of the pantheon. Through the decades I remained steadfast in my duties and devotion to this calling. And yes, teaching was—remains—my calling. I recall the Scottish author Sir James Barrie, whose family like mine, also attempted to persuade him to choose ministry, a calling of a different persuasion. Yet, from a young age, Sir James wished to forge a career as an author, just as I had wanted to be an academic since my days in short pants. I daresay, despite this grizzled head, I still harbor a desire no different than Peter Pan's, to live each passing year without growing older, not so that I may forever indulge in youthful hijinks, but so that I may continue to revisit great works of literature and share these treasures with my students.

I consider myself one of the lucky ones.

[Pause]

Or perhaps not.

They are all gone now. First, my mentor Otto O. Kendricks, who named me his successor as chair. He retreated from academia to write his memoirs but was felled by a stroke before completing volume one. Also gone, my closest colleagues—the "Wallys"—a pantheon unto ourselves. I count among my many blessings these dear friends, these scholars, these fellow faculty—Franklin, Preston, and DeMille. The four of us hailed from vastly different backgrounds (Franklin, a Harvard man; Preston and DeMille, both Princetonians; and myself, one of the Lords of Kenyon College). Together we soared through our salad days, celebrated our tenures, and enjoyed many a pint and late evening of rhetorical debate at the pub.

Oh, how I regret my later rift with DeMille, both of us men in our fifties, behaving like sentimental fools in our mutual vying for the attentions of sweet Millie, the widowed department secretary. DeMille, of course, won her heart. He was a silver-tongued master of English Romanticism and a bit of the dashing rebel with those sideburns. I should have graciously acknowledged him the more deserving suitor. Now it is too late for apologies. Cancer took Millie two decades ago, and DeMille's brilliant mind no longer recognizes a banana.

Ah, well. If C. S. Lewis is to be trusted—and who but a horse's ass would mistrust one of the most influential writers and intellectual giants of the twentieth century—then we can all take comfort in his words: *There are better things ahead than any we leave behind.* I expect it won't be too much longer before the Wallys—including me and that devilish, dashing DeMille—find ourselves reunited in that great English Department in the sky, greeting one another with our customary hail-fellow-well-met handshake.

[Pause]

Forgive my sentimentality. The awarding of the Walter S. Walters College "Distinguished Master Teacher Prize," er, the "Diversity Enhancement Award," warrants not tears, but smiles, for it represents the college's ongoing commitment to the humanities, even in the face of declining enrollment and the disheartening call for more "job-oriented" disciplines. In my own glory days, this coveted prize was bestowed upon me thrice, much to the dismay of my friendly rival Franklin, though the following year I was back again at this very podium, introducing him as my successor honoree. It is still hard to fathom, merely a decade after earning the title of Distinguished Master Teacher, that Franklin announced his retirement and retreated to his waterside cottage in Maine.

"Sailing to Byzantium." At our last pub gathering, Franklin raised a glass to the Wallys and offered up this toast to both his favorite poem, and to his retirement. Each of us raised our pints in return, reciting in unison the poem's opening line . . . "That is no country for old men."

Yeats. When other words fail, there is always Yeats.

[Pause]

But this evening is not about poets and professors of the past. As I look at all of you gathered here for this award ceremony, even these tired eyes can recognize a sea change of faces and attitudes. Please believe me when I tell you, despite my ancient form and fondness for tradition, I am not unhappy to witness the march of progress. The Wallys themselves were renegades in their own time.

[Pause . . . audience murmurs . . . a chair scraping]

Once again, forgive an old man his long memory and present shortcomings. My apologies, in particular, to this woman now standing beside me at the podium. It is indeed my special privilege to introduce her tonight, the newest recipient of the "Distinguished Master Teacher Prize," er, the "Diversity Enhancement Award." Thank you, my dear, for your steadying hand on my arm. Your presence is much appreciated.

But before I turn the podium over to my gifted colleague, indulge me one final reminiscence. I once had the immeasurable pleasure of meeting the remarkable English writer Sir Victor (V. S.) Pritchett, who is probably too far in the past for many of you to know. The prolific author begins one of his stories thusly: "The old man—but when does old age begin?—the old man turned over in bed and putting out his hand to the crest of his beautiful wife's white rising hip and comforting bottom, hit the wall with his knuckles and woke up."

I have no beautiful wife with a white rising hip and comforting bottom. Save for my brief enchantment with the fetching Millie, there were no sirens luring me to matrimony. Unlike the old man in Sir Victor's story, when I turn over in bed, my hand seeks a different form of comfort. Yet, my knuckles, too, hit the wall, as I reach for one of my own beloveds—Homer, Chaucer, Shakespeare—and realize that gone is the English Department of my yesteryear.

As I stand here now, supported both by this evening's worthy honoree, and by this familiar podium—a sturdy symbol of so many of my finest memories at Walter S. Walters College—I dare to presume your thoughts:

What place is there for an old man in the Department of Literatures?

Is such a relic even capable of changing with the times?

What has this professor to hope for, to anticipate, in his diminishing days at this institution he has long called home?

My dear colleagues and students, perhaps the answer to all three of these questions can be found in the person of our aspiring graduate Jesse Pepperidge and the delivery of the fifth draft of *their* thesis on *Coriolanus*, due on my desk next Friday at four.

~~

Conversation Interruptus

The summer birthday party was in full swing when I found myself standing across the kitchen counter from Naomi, a realtor I knew slightly, only because we'd both been to a couple of previous birthday parties at this same house. In truth, I usually avoided Naomi at these annual gatherings, mostly because she didn't seem the type to suffer fools, or at least that was the impression I got when I overheard her standing at the edge of the hosts' boat dock, snapping her wet hair as she lambasted some broker on the other end of her cell.

"I'm telling you, I've already got three cash offers over asking . . . Why? I'll tell you why. Because everyone and their rich uncle wants to move to goddamn Vermont after fucking COVID!"

But this afternoon, despite my intimidation, fate had thrown us together across the hummus platter.

"How's it going?" I said, an insufferable fool's beginning to a conversation if ever there was one. Fortunately, however, our exchange quickly took an interesting turn, as Naomi announced that her thirty-nine-year-old daughter had called her earlier that day to ask her a question—Would her mother (Naomi) be upset if she decided against having any kids?

"I told my daughter that I *never* wanted kids," Naomi continued, waving a baby carrot at me for emphasis. "I told her that getting pregnant was the *last* thing that I had ever wanted."

Wow. First, where did that burst of vehemence come from? Naomi and I had never even had a real conversation, let alone one at this level of intimacy. And second, naturally, I had some follow-up questions, such as: How did her daughter respond to such unmotherly news? Was the girl taken aback by the fact that, according to her own mom, her conception was so unwelcome that it even trumped other negative consequences of intercourse, say the clap or genital warts.

Naomi's disclosure seemed like the type of truth bomb that might devastate a child, even a thirty-nine-year-old child, and commit them to therapy for life. But before I could find out how the rest of Naomi's conversation with her daughter had played out, the hostess of the party came into the kitchen with a birthday cake full of lit candles, people started singing, cake was served, and Naomi abandoned me to mingle among less insufferable party-goers.

I've noticed this happens a lot during social gatherings—a conversation will just be getting started, only to be waylaid by some distraction, often inconsequential, and that's the end of that story, even if the person has just shared something deeply personal or significant.

"My doctor told me this morning I have six weeks to live."

"Oh look, Maggie and Quentin just arrived . . . and she's brought her world-famous guacamole dip!"

After my truncated conversation with Naomi, I suppose I could have chased her down during the party and interrupted whatever new conversation she was having with the next person—"Excuse me, Naomi! Naomi! Remember back in the kitchen when you were telling me how you had told your daughter that you *never* wanted kids? Was she okay with that? What did she say? What happened next?" But I didn't chase down Naomi at the party because, let's face it, when a conversational moment passes, that kind of backtracking can just feel awkward.

I'm sure my attention span is as fleeting as most people's in today's TikTok world but it bugs me, all these loose threads from unfinished stories. Sometimes it's the speaker herself who drifts away without finishing her thought. Sometimes, more often, it's the listener who becomes distracted. I've coined a term for this modern malady—*Conversation*

Interruptus—translated from the Latin to mean that if someone says something to you like, "I saw my dead mother standing at the end of my bed last night . . ." or "I just learned the FBI bugged my offices . . ." there's something wrong with you if you don't stop texting, ignore the cat encircling your legs, resist the urge to cut in with your own run-in with the FBI, and pay attention to the rest of their story.

And as much as I dislike when others are interrupted, I absolutely hate it when someone interrupts my train of thought. Here is just one recent example.

"I just got the first review of my new book!" I announced to my good friend Jason, as soon as we had grabbed a couple of seats at our favorite dive bar. "And it's really good!"

"Hey, look!" Jason pointed his chin in the direction of a distinctive-looking man at the end of the bar. "I think that's Sylvester Stallone!"

Celebrity sightings do rank high on my short list of worthy interruptions, especially given their rarity in White River Junction, Vermont. But puhleeze. One glance at this stranger was enough to see that maybe, sort of, this droopy-eyed, dark-haired man looked close enough to Sylvester Stallone to be his stunt double. But hadn't Jason heard what I had just said? *I just got my first rave review!* I understand how everyone, including me, is sick of authors and their shameless self-promotion, but Jason is my friend. He's obligated to listen to my bragging and pretend to care. But instead of congratulating me, we spent the next twenty minutes whisper-debating whether this stranger really was Sylvester Stallone, and why someone worth 400 million dollars would be at this dive bar. And, yes, I could have returned to the subject of my book review, but I didn't because I was testing Jason. *He* should have been the one to pick up that loose thread, and then he should get his eyes checked.

Of course, like the saying goes, things could always be worse. Or at least different. I remember when I was first married to my ex-husband, Steve. Back then, Steve was a psychologist in training, along with most of our friends at the time. I'm sure it was a function of these doctoral students being new to their field, but they didn't just listen, they *actively* listened. We'd all be hanging around watching a football game or playing trivia, and I'd make a comment like, "I hate the way these Cheetos turn my fingers orange," to which one or the other would respond:

"So what I'm hearing is that having stains on your fingers can be upsetting."

"Do you have issues with the color orange? Does it make you think of prison? Are you worried you might go to prison?"

"*Hate* is a strong word. Let's talk about that some more at next week's game."

It used to annoy the bejesus out of me, feeling like these aspiring therapists were practicing on me, even when we were just socializing. Funny though, now when I think back on that time, I remember how one of the things that had attracted me to Steve in the first place was the way he paid attention; the way he took me seriously; the way he didn't get distracted by birthday cake.

By the time Steve and I got divorced over two decades later, it was hard to untangle whether, at some point, Steve had stopped listening or I had stopped talking, or maybe it was the other way around. I'm not sorry my ex and I are no longer together, and I'm grateful that we've remained good friends, but that doesn't mean that I don't have regrets. In fact, if I was going to put on my own therapist hat, I might point out that "regrets" is a strong word, and what I'm hearing myself say is that, when I was married, I should have been more appreciative of all that effort that goes into active listening.

It could be because I am a writing instructor or naturally nosy, but when someone like me is left with a loose thread, I'm the type of person who will tug on it. So, let's see, where had Naomi left me hanging in the story she'd been telling me from across the hummus platter? That's right, she'd just announced to her thirty-nine-year-old daughter that she'd never wanted any children. So what happened next? Well, since I didn't hear it from Naomi, you'll hear it from me, or at least how the story played out in my mind.

Not long after that conversation Naomi's daughter got pregnant accidentally on purpose. The new mother named the baby after its grandmother, the grandmother on the *other* side of the family, the one whom Naomi had never liked. Then the new family of three moved far away from Vermont (bucking the post-COVID trend to move here), and Naomi was deeply disappointed. And while Naomi did receive a

Christmas card from them every year, the gesture sent a certain message, mostly because Naomi is Jewish.

But why? Why had Naomi's daughter turned against her? In the years that followed, Naomi found herself asking this question countless times. They used to be so close. She misses her girl. And she misses the grandchild she has yet to meet, not unlike the way you might miss a phantom limb. Then one day in the far future, Naomi, alone and sad, her real estate license long expired, recalls that phone call with her daughter, the one where she'd announced that she never wanted kids. Too late, Naomi realizes that this was the moment when everything went wrong.

"I never wanted children . . . *until I had you.*" That last crucial clause is what I imagine Naomi had intended to add, until the conversation got interrupted over something trivial, maybe the doorbell, maybe a birthday cake. But of course now if Naomi tried to explain this to her daughter, or even to me, it would sound like backtracking; too little too late. It's such a shame, to see a mother estranged from her daughter, but when you leave it to others to pick up where you left off, the end of your story just might not turn out the way that you'd hoped.

Lambies in Jammies!

Recently I read an article about researchers in neurobiology who discovered that mice have micro expressions. In humans—and apparently in rodents—micro expressions are those little facial giveaways that reveal our true emotions. Unlike our macro expressions that we consciously control to either match what we're saying—or use to try and cover up what we're really thinking and feeling—our micro expressions happen without our knowledge and in a flash.

There! For one-fifteenth of a second, your boss flashed the upper whites of his eyeballs. You knew it! He may be trying to appear as supercilious as ever, but micro expressions do not lie. What he just revealed was fear—fear that you might actually hit him with that stapler you are using to collate his stupid 391-page, double-sided annual report. Examples of other micro expressions:

A glimpse of horizontal wrinkles across the forehead: surprise.

A fast flair of nostrils: anger.

Crow's feet when you smile: real happiness (versus a fake smile that fails to engage the side eye muscles).

And the hardest micro expression of all to fake: sadness, which we involuntarily reveal by drawing in and then up the inner corners of the eyebrows.

Out of curiosity I went to the mirror and tried to make my eyebrows look sad, but I don't think they bend that way. At least not when I am consciously trying to do so.

The neurobiologists who determined that mice have the same seven universal micro expressions as humans (disgust, anger, fear, sadness, happiness, surprise, and contempt) did so by hooking up the little creatures to a machine that can register their facial expressions on a timescale of milliseconds. Thanks to the wonders of two-photon microscopy, the researchers could even measure the intensity of the emotion by comparing it to the neuronal activity in the mice's relevant brain areas. Take two little mice. One has a full tummy. One is hungry. When each was given sugar water, they both reacted with micro expressions of happiness (if you can imagine such cuteness), but the thirsty mouse's neurons registered a greater intensity of happiness than the brain activity of the non-thirsty mouse.

Normally, I like learning about these kinds of out-of-the-ordinary scientific studies, one reason being that they serve as good icebreakers at parties.

"Did you know that scientists have found that it is just as easy to swim in maple syrup as in water?"

"Have you read the studies that determined chickens prefer to peck at people considered beautiful?"

"Perhaps you've heard that research has shown that sitting at the back, but not the front, of a rollercoaster can dislodge kidney stones. But of course the real question is how do you convince someone with kidney stones to go to a theme park?"

What stranger wouldn't want to talk to me at a party after those kinds of conversation starters? But this discovery about mice having micro expressions didn't sit right with me, not at all. It suggested that these little creatures might be more complicated than meets the eye. To the uneducated, they may simply look cute, but what if their micro expressions—too fleeting and small to register with the naked eye—belied a less pleasant truth: that underneath all that adorableness they weren't feeling cute at all, but rather were mad, or scared, or sad.

I hate the thought of a sad mouse—or a sad anything with fur or fluff or paws. I have always felt tenderly toward animals, even those that would eat me. Through the years I have anthropomorphized all my pets and treat my current precious Kitty like a tiny baby, cradling her in my arms and carrying on conversations with her while speaking both our parts.

"You love your Mommy, right Kitty?"

"Oh yes, Mommy, you are the best Mommy in the world."

I need to take Kitty's adorable features—her round green eyes, her soft fur, her little grey nose—at face value. I need to believe that she and every other cute animal in the world is just that—cute—because these creatures are the one and only thing that can offer instant solace in a world overwhelmed by horrific headlines.

Domestic Terrorism on Rapid Rise!

Aww. A teacup pig drinking from a baby bottle.

Studies Warn of Multiple Famines of Biblical Proportions!

Just look at how those rescued elephants cuddle with their keepers.

Climate Crisis Threatens Mass Extinction!

Ha, ha, ha. A cockatoo perched on the edge of the couch, rocking out to Springsteen.

While research into the micro expressions in mice is new, the study of these unconscious facial signals in humans is a much more established practice. Most notably, FBI profilers read micro expressions to help them suss out liars and serial killers. Mentalists, too, use their ability to read these fleeting facial giveaways in order to fool people into thinking they are actually psychic. Some experts go so far as to describe micro expressions as "windows to the soul" and claim that the ability to discern them is akin to having a superpower, like being able to read someone's mind.

According to a national poll, mind-reading is the superpower that Americans would most like to have—tied with the ability to time travel—but personally speaking, no thank you! The last thing I would want is someone reading my mind (where they would find a whole lot of self-soothing counting going on). Plus, I do not want to know what other people are really thinking, especially about me, because whenever I have eavesdropped on certain conversations where I am the topic, that has rarely turned out as well as I had hoped.

On the other hand, I imagine how the world might be different if people's true thoughts were on full display, open to anyone with the ability to track the curve of an eyebrow or the flicker of a lip. Would it prevent the rise of future psychopaths if their followers saw clearly into their dark souls, assuming psychopaths even have souls? Would it expose the duplicity of the psychopath's enablers who plaster on macro expressions that show deference, while their micro expressions are screaming, "WTF, *you batshit boil?!*"

Evil Regime Ushers in New Reign of Cruelty and Inhumanity!

So precious, lambies in jammies.

Swarm of Drones Could Obliterate America's Infrastructure!

Be still my heart. A yawning lop-eared bunny.

Surging Mutant Viruses Overtake the World!

Whee! See how the pandas tussle and tumble in the snow.

Even me, who is equally skeptical of that other most coveted super-power—time travel—can understand the desire to escape these modern headlines; to escape to a time, or place, or world away from one where misery seems to be multiplying by the minute. This is why I need daily hits of pure, unadulterated cuteness. This is why I think we need to inundate the Internet with cute animal videos, just to remind ourselves that some things, even in the face of pandemics and global unrest, and massacres, and gross racial injustices remain as pure and sweet as sunbathing seals, and gorillas hugging, and penguins playing tag. This is why I think those nosy neuroscientists with their mouse microscopy should have left well enough alone.

I roam my condo until I find my cat, taking a nap in her favorite rocker in my daughter's bedroom. My precious Kitty is the living embodiment of a cute animal video; her softness and throaty purr serve as instant balms to my soul.

"You don't have micro expressions, do you?" I pick her up and cradle her soft plumpness.

"Oh no, Mommy!" Kitty answers in that adorable, high-pitched voice she uses whenever we have our many conversations. "I'm the happiest Kitty in the world!"

I squeeze her tight and kiss her all over her furry head. Pure love emanates from her big green eyes. Her adorable round face never fails to make me smile. Maybe if I looked closer, I would see how one side of Kitty's mouth twitches upward in a flash of contempt, the only one of the seven micro expressions that is asymmetrical. I might even be able to detect my own hidden feelings in the inward and upward tilt of my eyebrows. Sadness, the hardest emotion to fake. But why would I want to go there, to that darker, weary world? Why would I want to open that window when I can simply bury my face in Kitty's soft fur, let her purr resonate through my chest, and enjoy this moment of respite?

Testing Negative

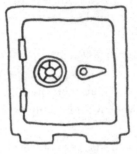

Over the years, Helmut has told me on several occasions that I have a vault inside my head where I store every wrong, hurt, insult, and slight I've ever suffered or imagined. The first time he mentioned this we were with friends and the subject came up of how we met.

"We met in a bar, but on our first real date—or what was *supposed* to be our first real date—Helmut stood me up," I told the others. "I was really looking forward to it, too, when he texted me that he was sick." I air quoted the last word—"sick"—for effect. This was hardly the first time I had shared this story, so by now I knew exactly how to play it for maximum effect.

"But I was sick," Helmut put up a pathetic defense.

"You had a little sniffle," I dismissed his argument with a wave of my hand. "Plus, if you were really interested, you would have kept the date even if you were on death's door." As proof of his cold feet, I pointed out that he hadn't even bothered to contact me again, and we might never have gotten together except I spotted him at the farmer's market well over a year later, and I approached *him*. Lucky for Helmut, I was in a magnanimous mood thanks to the sunshine, and the fact that I'd just moved into my own place after my divorce. Also, he looked adorable, sitting alone at a picnic table, eating a messy Mexican wrap. We left the market together, and he came home with me to see my new place, where he made short work of fixing my broken garbage disposal. That, of course, was only one reason why I quickly fell in love with him and asked him to move in with me six months later.

When Helmut first told me I had a vault inside my head, it gave me pause. I hadn't realized it until that moment, but I am indeed like Wells Fargo, only instead of safekeeping rare coins and important documents, my vault contains a lifetime of carefully preserved, time-stamped grievances, which I withdraw when the occasion suits. A few examples:

Near the back of the vault, fifth grade: One of my schoolmates, whom I'd assumed was a friend, failed to invite me to her big pool-party-slash-sleepover. Now, every time her sixty-year-old face pops up on Facebook in the section "People you may know," my first reaction is, *Well, I thought I knew her, but I guess I had it wrong.*

Tucked away from fourteen years ago: In a conversation with my beloved niece, I shared with her that a psychic who specializes in past lives had told me that this was my "lucky life." To this she responded with visible incredulity, *"This is your lucky life?"* I adore my niece, but who could forget such a reaction of disbelief?

And fresh to the vault: The other week I ran into a friend and her second husband. The man is an actor, and they divide their time between Vermont and Los Angeles. "Nice to meet you," the man greeted me, even though we've met 70 billion times before. I'm not saying I'm going to stop watching reruns of the television series where he played a brilliant but troubled surgeon for six seasons, but from now on when I see him on the screen, I'll probably withdraw this little deposit and another memory along with it—of my friend telling me that when she and her second husband were first dating, her mother thought he was way too old for her.

It's been estimated that sixty-five thousand thoughts pass through our minds on any given day. If that is true, then my vault was clearly where

I stored a cache of the bad ones. But even outside my vault, my head contained other categories of negativity—complaints, tirades, revenge fantasies—that didn't merit space in the vault, but did seem to occupy a good part of my mentalscape, and often leaked into my conversation:

> "What is the deal with all these roundabouts? Just give me a good old-fashioned traffic light!"

> "Wouldn't it be great if I replaced all the flowers in my snobby neighbor's window boxes with plastic ones from Family Dollar!"

> "Those damn fundraisers for firefighters and the police. It should be illegal to call people after six!"

Because sixty-five thousand thoughts a day seemed like a lot, I figured there must be a lot of wiggle room before the more vengeful or nasty thoughts threw shade over your entire personality. Or one would hope. But apparently I had figured wrong, because over the past few years a chorus of people—meaning most of my family and friends—had started saying things to me like:

"Don't be so negative."

"Don't be so negative."

"Okay, okay, we get it. You don't like roundabouts. Have you seen my noise-cancelling headphones?"

Normally, when I'm in the throes of complaining, someone telling me "Don't be so negative" goes over about as well as when a stranger walks by and tells me to "Smile." (*You smile, asshole!*) But this comment kept coming at me from people I knew and loved; people who spent a lot of time with me. I couldn't ignore them, and finally, after being told not to be so negative for what seemed like the umpteenth time, I came to understand what these loved ones were actually trying to tell me, which was this: *Don't be so negative!*

But how did this happen? And to me, of all people? For most of my life I have been characterized as the quintessential youngest child—social, upbeat, creative, and good at getting other people to do things for her. "Oh Joni, you like everyone!" I didn't like everyone, of course, but I do know I used to be a lot more positive, prone to some mood swings maybe, but they quickly passed. The decline of my disposition could be attributed to any number of things—aging, all but two Republicans in Congress, the way almond milk refuses to properly froth—but whatever the cause, it was clear my negativity had evolved from a transitory trait to a personality type in the form of a proper noun. I had become a Negative Person.

Shortly after I realized I was a Negative Person, I experienced another upsetting revelation. I was probably dying. Or so I had convinced myself because I had developed a swath of symptoms that defied easy diagnosis, at least over the Internet. (*Why couldn't my symptoms resemble something like ringworm, with its trademark ring-shaped rash?*) When I put on a sports bra, I noticed that my right breast felt tender, like it had been stung by a horsefly, only there was no discernable lump or bite mark. Also, my stomach ached after every meal, and most days I felt bone tired, starting about forty minutes after I woke up These symptoms were all iterations of things I'd previously experienced and simply waited out, partly because I hated going to the doctor, and partly because I believed they would pass. But that wishful thinking only worked before I had become a Negative Person.

For years, I had read about the physical and psychological payoffs of positivity and gratitude. This was the one point on which Western and Eastern medicine seemed to heartily agree. In contrast, not once had I read about the health benefits of lugging around a mental vault of grievances, or occupying your free time by plotting revenge. Logically, I understood that people didn't die of negativity. Disease, sadly, is indiscriminate; the good die young, and some of the most evil fucks in the world never seem to keel over. Still, I couldn't shake the thought—being a Negative Person was not only a terrible diagnosis unto itself, but put me at much higher risk for all sorts of health issues. I figured it was like stress—it wouldn't kill me outright, but after I died my Negative Soul would look down at my fresh corpse, a complaint still written on my blue lips, and make a point to rub it in. *"I told you so."*

It was this frame of mind that forced me, reluctantly, to visit my primary care doctor, whom I hadn't seen in five years, according to the records in my patient portal. Hence her eagerness to drain me of blood while she had the chance. Based on my complaints, the doctor sent six vials to the lab, where my blood was tested for levels of B12, C-reactive protein, folate, TSH, anti-tissue transglutaminase antibodies, and on and on. Within days, I learned that I would not be dying in the immediate future, at least not from inflammation, diabetes, thyroid and liver disease, anemia, hypertension, or gluten sensitivity.

Later that same week, I also got the results of the mammogram my doctor had ordered, which indicated that my scans came back "normal." Normal! Just reading that good news was enough to forget the horsefly bite on my right breast (which had already vanished anyway). I'd been given a reprieve! A gift! The miracle of good health!

I posted the results of my mammogram and the results of my blood work on my fridge, reminders of my good fortune. Here was hard proof—I had been screened for virtually everything so I had absolutely nothing to complain about! In rereading the letter about my mammogram, I did notice a typo, but this would be my first opportunity for change. From this moment forward I would not be so critical. I would stop dwelling on past wrongs and plotting revenge. I would find my way back to my inner youngest child—social, upbeat, creative, and good at getting others to do things for her.

"We're starting a gratitude journal," I alerted Helmut. This was a few weeks after I'd posted my mammogram and all my lab results on the fridge. Despite my resolve, it had become clear that, being a Negative Person, I'd have to work twice as hard to shed my negativity, plus I needed all the support I could get. "Every day you write something in the gratitude journal that you appreciate about me and I'll do the same for you," I explained. "I'll leave it on the back of the toilet in the downstairs bathroom so neither of us will forget." Experts in the field of positive psychology have long touted the transformative effects of writing down a daily dose of gratitude, so I figured that Helmut and I could do this together, even though he already had enough positivity for the both of us.

I appreciate how Helmut makes such lovely meals.

I'm grateful Helmut works out and takes care of himself.

I like hearing Helmut play piano.

Faithfully, I made my daily entries. As the pages filled, I resisted the urge to reread what had been written, wanting to savor the entries from a more distant perspective. Then one afternoon several months later, the time felt right so I took the gratitude journal to the couch, opening it to random pages.

I appreciate when Helmut brings me coffee in the morning.

I'm thankful Helmut fills the bird feeders.

I love Helmut's creativity and imagination.

It was meaningful to see in black and white how grateful I was for Helmut. Maybe I was actually starting to change, I thought. A Negative Person wouldn't have written all those nice things about her boyfriend, not because they weren't true, but because she never would have noticed. I flipped backwards through the pages, looking for Helmut's entries about me. Finally, near the front of the journal, I stumbled upon a single entry.

I'm grateful that Joni made the bed this morning.

Really? I thought. Sixty-five thousand thoughts on any given day, and that's the best you got? Quickly, I chided myself—Don't be so negative. By now, I didn't need others to tell me that I needed to change my personality, though I did need to keep telling myself. Even in the face of good fortune, even with a daily dose of gratitude, it was still too easy to revert to type. Sometimes it felt like it would take a miracle to get me to stop being so negative —except that I'd already been given a miracle when it turned out that I wasn't dying.

On the way to the powder room to return the gratitude journal to its rightful place on the toilet, I stopped at the fridge, its door still displaying my mammogram report, along with the results of my blood-work. One more time, I read through the long list of components in my blood—vitamins, protein, minerals, glucose— that all had tested negative for any problems. I remained clueless how urea nitrogen helped or hurt a liver, but what mattered was that mine had a value of fourteen, which was well within the normal range. So why get upset, I told myself, that the only thing Helmut had written in our shared journal was that he was grateful I had made the bed.

With that in mind, I returned the gratitude journal—along with Helmut's single, lame comment—back to its place on the tank of the toilet, but not before some Negative Person had managed to slip yet another grievance into my vault.

My Four-Mile Run

The Official, Ordinary Tour

Welcome to ordinary citizen Joni B. Cole's most frequent running route, a four-mile, partially paved path located just a stone's throw (and quick dash across Route 5) from her condo. Be sure to visit each of these eight everyday attractions along the path, plus read on to learn some of the usual thoughts Joni has as she runs by these sites.

1. D. B. ELEMENTARY SCHOOL

Joni's route starts at the home of 254 little Hartford Hurricanes! In what seems like a lifetime ago, Joni's two daughters attended D. B. Elementary School, which is why it evokes so many feelings of motherhood. Whenever she runs by this school, Joni can't help but think: *They grow up so fast . . . except they don't. Not in your mind. Not in your heart.*

The other month, Joni had a dream in which her younger daughter, now in her twenties, was back in second grade, dressed like Amelia Earhart in a bomber jacket and aviator hat. This was the same outfit she wore in real life when her class put on a show called "Favorite Figures from History."

"My name is Amelia Earhart. I was the first female aviator to fly solo across the Atlantic . . ." In the dream, Joni's girl recites the same lines she spoke during the actual performance, but then the dream turned into a nightmare.

A gunman bursts into the auditorium!

"You owe me for the heroin!" he aims his weapon. "Get me twenty-six thousand dollars by midnight or else."

In the nightmare, Joni's daughter—who is somehow both a little girl and a young adult at the same time—gives her mother a reassuring look, her eyes a calming blue. *It's okay. I'll be fine.* But Joni doesn't have twenty-six thousand dollars to give to this man aiming a type of gun that shouldn't even exist in a sane world, let alone an elementary school. How is she supposed to keep her daughter safe?

In real life, her daughter has never bought heroin, and she has never been the victim of a school shooting. She is all grown up and has proven herself more than capable. But a mother still feels compelled to issue warnings.

"Be careful!"

"Remember, go for an assailant's knees! Stab his eyes! Yank his earlobes!"

"Have fun, sweetie, and pack that pepper spray!"

But what good would this kind of maternal vigilance do anyway? The world keeps spinning in crazy directions, so even someone as capable as Amelia Earhart can just end up . . . gone.

Sometimes when Joni runs by the elementary school playground, a child will let out a high laugh or scream, and she has to press a hand to her heart to stop its pounding. It helps to recall her daughter's calming blue eyes from the dream. These young students—and her own two girls—they'll be all right, she tells herself, because how else do you get through a day? But, really, how can a mother ever relax, when even an elementary school can act like a trigger?

2. THE HIPPIE HOMESTEAD

On any given day, you're likely to hear seventies music coming from somewhere on this unconventional property boasting a weathered house and barn, an above-ground pool, a trash-barrel fire-pit, and a peaceable kingdom of barnyard animals! Goats. Turkeys. Geese. A pot-bellied pig. Plus, chickens, lots of chickens that like to scooch under the bent wire fence separating the homestead from the path. If you're jogging, be careful you don't run a-fowl!

Joni loves animals but wants nothing to do with chickens because she eats them. Indeed, chicken is the only meat she still reluctantly consumes, and if she gave that up she'd need to eat more beans, which would be difficult because she's no fan of legumes. Plus, she knows what a pain it is to have picky eaters over for dinner, and doesn't want to be one of those guests, even though she already, sort of, is that guest.

Joni admits she is stymied by how many of her friends have started raising chickens for fun, building them elaborate roosts and letting them peck around their lawns. These friends aren't farmers or homesteaders; in fact many of them are writers with active imaginations, and it doesn't take much imagination to envision those buffalo wings on your plate flapping around in search of their missing bodies.

Under protest, she has listened to all the arguments in favor of raising chickens, with a reliable source of fresh eggs being only one of them.

"Chickens have great personalities."

"Chickens take care of pests and help clean up the garden."

"Chickens are cheap and don't need to be walked or groomed."

"Chickens are awesome if you have young children."

One of her friends even has a chicken as a house pet. ("Henny sleeps with my daughter every night!")

When Joni runs past the hippie homestead and its fence decorated with American flags, she likes hearing the music blaring from the speakers. She also likes how these people with the menagerie are just doing their thing (despite some grumbles from neighbors about zoning violations). Lots of times, the friendly homesteaders leave a cooler of free bottled water for the joggers and fill a bucket for the pooches. What's the big deal, Joni thinks, having to dodge a few Rhode Island Reds and Plymouth Rocks as they strut across the path? She just wishes when they do, she wouldn't imagine taking a bite out of their thighs.

3. THE SPLOTCH OF COMMITMENT

Unless you are closely following every footfall, it's unlikely you'll even notice this small splotch of paint on the pavement. Under different circumstances, such a splotch wouldn't even qualify as a Rorschach reject, but the fact that it falls exactly one mile from Joni's house is what earns it the status of landmark.

The Splotch of Commitment marks the point of no excuses. When reached, it signifies that Joni cannot, under any circumstances, cut short her four-mile run in either direction. She cannot stop to rest. She cannot walk. She must keep running, even if she is struggling, even if her music cuts out and all she can hear is the slow thud of her own footfalls.

What happens, you may be wondering, if Joni ignores the power she has invested in the Splotch of Commitment, established solely for the purpose of keeping her motivated. Ah, well, Joni makes sure this doesn't happen by instituting different cosmic consequences depending on the day and the degree of her flagging energy.

If I stop running I will break my foot tripping over an acorn. Yes, an acorn, for added humiliation!

If I stop running I will never get published again.

If I stop running I will quickly slide down that slippery slope where I start thinking it's okay to not bother, to cut corners, to quit.

One particularly difficult run last winter, Joni slowed as she approached the Splotch of Commitment. She felt horrible, and not in the usual way that first mile can feel like you're dragging a piano. One step forward . . . two steps . . . the toe of her sneaker touched the white paint. Now there was no turning back!

If I stop running I will quickly slide down that slippery slope where I start thinking it's okay to not bother, to cut corners, to quit.

This cosmic consequence, the second most extreme, had always been intended to prevent one of Joni's worst fears—that one day she will just stop doing stuff because, why the hell not? It would be so much easier to be that person, except that she doesn't want to be that person. Some days, it seems, the only thing between her and that lazy quitter is the Splotch of Commitment and its cosmic consequences.

But on this particular run, such was her lack of energy that even this consequence didn't feel like enough motivation to keep her feet moving forward. *Don't go there*, she thought. *Don't even think it!* But in her weakened condition, the most extreme cosmic consequence—the one she vowed she would never employ given its implications—forced its way into her head:

If I stop running I'll die!

Thank goodness, Joni completed that run (though her pace on the last hill looked a lot like walking). Of course, she knows that some people think it's silly, naming a paint mark on the running path the Splotch of Commitment, and believing that cosmic consequences can keep us in line. She also knows that on that day she didn't die after her horrible run, but she did come down with the worst case of the flu she has ever suffered, which just goes to show, the cosmos knows the difference between running and walking, so don't think it isn't paying attention.

4. STONY CREEK CONDOMINIUMS

This multiunit residential complex is made up of two- and three-bedroom homes, each featuring a spacious living area (with a gas fireplace!) and a small yard and deck for entertaining. When Joni was going through a divorce several years ago, she looked at one of these condos for her and her two growing girls. But how in the world did one actually go about achieving such a dream—a place of one's own—especially on a writing teacher's earnings?

Stony Creek is not where Joni ended up, but soon after her divorce, she did manage to buy a condo only a mile or so away, which also has three bedrooms, a gas fireplace, and a little yard. Much of that tumultuous period in her life is a blur, but she still remembers the challenges of getting a mortgage, and the creativity and kindness of one particular mortgage lender. But, truly, even with the loan figures available in black and white, how this miracle happened remains as much a mystery as math.

Not too long ago, a new neighbor bought the condo on the other side of Joni's wall, their places mirror images. One day, the woman popped over to introduce herself.

"Don't you find it hard to live in a place so small?" she asked Joni.

Apparently, this new neighbor, single with grown children, had down-sized and was having second thoughts.

"Doesn't the noise from all the traffic bother you?" she pointed out Joni's windows facing Route 5, located just on the other side of her condo's little yard with a picket fence.

"You'd think there would be more room for gardens," the new neighbor added. By now, Joni wished she had never answered the door. Before she left, the woman surveyed Joni's sparsely decorated living room and empty wall space. "Aren't you planning to hang any art?"

When Joni runs by the Stony Brook Condominiums, it takes her back to that time when the dream of owning her own gas fireplace seemed like an impossibility. Not once, since she moved into her own condo, has she ever felt it was too small, even when she was living with two teenagers. She rarely notices the sounds of traffic on the other side of her picket fence, and she can't imagine a more perfect garden than the single row of flowers along her walkway, all planted and cared for by the boyfriend she found the very weekend she moved into her new home.

Profluence, Joni thinks. Forwardmovingness. Somehow, she managed to emerge from that painful period of her divorce with a place of her own—a tabula rasa to accommodate a future of possibilities. No wonder, even all these years later, Joni still remains reluctant to clutter up her walls or cede any of her precious space.

5. LITTLE TIMBER FOOTBRIDGE

Perhaps the most scenic spot on the route, this little wooden footbridge arches over a trickle of a stream and is bordered on one side by a patch of woodlands. Here is the perfect place to appreciate the natural beauty of Vermont, despite the fact you are less than a mile away from a mini mart! Indeed, anywhere in the Green Mountain State, you can quickly find yourself in the woods, given 80 percent of Vermont is forested.

Thwack. Thwack. To Joni's ear, the sound of her footfalls crossing the timber bridge mimics the strike of an ax, which makes her recall Vermont's history with trees. She thinks about how, in the eighteenth century, the first European settlers started clearing the land for sheep farms; the more pastures the more room for flocks, and the more money to be made! When the sheep craze slowed near the end of the Civil War, loggers showed up and clear-cut more forest land to accommodate the railroads, and feed the huge demand for wood from the paper companies.

Thwack. Thwack. Over time, all this indiscriminate cutting spelled doom for those Vermonters who counted on the forest for their livelihood. The deforestation also led to soil erosion, dead fish, and barren hillsides that didn't give Vermont's tourist industry much to brag about. In 1889, the year the logging industry peaked, over 80 percent of the state had been cleared of trees, with few to be found below two thousand feet, which means the view from this little footbridge would have looked quite different back then.

Thwack. Thwack. Joni is always gobsmacked by how ignorant humans can be; how much damage they can inflict when motivated by money. But even more gobsmacking is how Vermont got its act together, thanks to a bunch of environmentalists, state legislators, and wealthy donors who worked together to seed the beginnings of what is now the Green Mountain National Forest, and an advanced forest policy.

Thwack, Thwack. So many of today's problems—climate change, to name one—feel hopeless. Irreversible. But the sound of Joni's footfalls on the little timber bridge serves to lift her spirits and offers a reminder: if a state can go from 80 percent treeless to 80 percent forested in just over a century, then maybe, just maybe, there's still reason to hope.

6. THE BLACK LEATHER GLOVE

Since last winter, this lone glove has rested on the grassy embankment next to the path. For Joni, it brings to mind another black leather glove made famous decades ago. That other glove was found outside O. J. Simpson's home after his estranged wife, Nicole Brown Simpson, had been stabbed seven times in the neck and scalp, and had her throat slashed. She died alongside another victim of the attack, twenty-five-year-old Ronald Goldman. Both had defensive wounds on their hands.

That black leather glove—the one found on O. J.'s property—turned out to be a perfect match to its mate at the murder scene. That glove showed traces of blood from both O. J. and the victims. That glove became much of the focus during O. J.'s nearly nine-month trial, along with other physical and circumstantial evidence, including his recent purchase of a stiletto knife, his shoe prints at the crime scene, Nicole's blood on a pair of socks at his house, and several reported instances of past abuse. During the trial a witness recounted how O. J. had told Nicole that one day he would "kill her and get away with it," and it appears that is exactly what happened.

But that was that black leather glove and here, on the grass next to the running path, is a glove just like it . . . only different. *Whose glove is this?* Joni often wonders as she jogs past it. What tale does it have to tell? Since the glove showed up last winter, she's imagined lots of possibilities, but here is just one of those stories:

"Where the heck is my other glove?" Ben asks his wife, Elise. The couple have been married nineteen years and have a daughter and a son. Ben looks under the couch for the umpteenth time. Elise loads the last dinner plate into the dishwasher. She's used to her sweetie misplacing things—his keys, his gym bag, the Valentine's Day card he bought her and forgot where he put it (under her pillow). But if being disorganized is his biggest fault, she can't complain, especially when she thinks about how willing he is to take Jennie out for her driving lessons or cart Benji to swim practice at five-thirty every morning.

"Honey," she says, "you've been looking for that glove for weeks. Let's just buy you another pair." He stands with a groan. All those school years and weekends playing ice hockey didn't do his knees any favors.

"But Jennie got me those gloves for Christmas," Ben argues. "They're my fancy pair." Elise smiles. She was with their daughter at the mall when Jennie bought her dad the gloves. They're pleather and cost twenty bucks. Elise isn't about to spoil the illusion. She loves how Ben acts like they're fancy, which they are compared to his beat-up work gloves.

"Jennie will forgive you." She kisses Ben's cheek, then hands him the kitchen trash bag to take to the bin.

In Joni's imagination, this black leather glove—the one in the grass by the running path—is the contronym of the one found at O. J. Simpson's house.

That glove—the one at the crime scene—shows that men get away with abusing and murdering their spouses. It shows that people are going to believe whatever they want to believe, despite all evidence. And it proves that there are some real sickos out there in the world who will never be brought to justice.

This glove—the one in the grass—serves as evidence that men love their wives and look after their families. It shows that people might willfully believe something that is untrue—like, say, pleather is as fancy as leather—but only because it holds sentimental value. This glove, Joni is reminded every time she runs past it on the path, proves that the world is still full of plenty of good guys, willing to take out the garbage.

7. THE INCLINE

This paved, upward stretch on the running route measures 1.2 miles and can feel much longer and steeper, depending on the weather and other variables, like how much sleep or wine happened the previous night. When Joni is struggling to make it up this hill, she distracts herself with a practice she's coined "mindfulness-over-macadam." Thoughts in. Thoughts out.

I can't believe some people still double-space after a period.

How come we admire people who get up early . . . but not people who stay up late?

How could anyone be a surgeon?

Thank God for surgeons.

Are people who make their bed every morning really more successful?

When someone says, "It's all downhill from here," is that a good thing or a bad thing?

I wish I was heading downhill.

Why are all the promos that show up when I open my Kindle for books like Lucifer's Mistress *or* The Princess's Passion. *Does Kindle really think that's the type of stuff I like to read?*

It should be illegal for people to drive with dogs on their laps.

I love my cat so much.

My legs feel like lead.

I wish I had an Australian accent.

It's weird I don't get poison ivy.

Why do hospital gift shops always sell jewelry?

I can't believe that exorcisms are on the rise.

Man, this hill is long.

If I stop running, I will trip over an acorn and break my foot.

If I stop running, I will never get published again.

If I stop running, I will quickly slide down that slippery slope where I start thinking it's okay to not bother, to cut corners, to quit.

I want to stop running. I'm going to stop running.

If I stop running, I'll die. No! I take it back! I take it back! But I can't take it back because the cosmos is always listening, and this time it won't settle for just giving me the flu!

8. GEORGIE'S GRAVE

You won't find an official marker, just a shady spot under the hedge that separates Joni's condominium complex from the neighboring cemetery. But here, at the base of the third tree in the row, lies Georgie, beloved first cat of Joni and Helmut, a topaz-eyed tabby and artful dodger, save for that last car traveling too fast down Route 5. Gone too soon, sweet Georgie boy. R.I.P.

Joni ends every run with the same ritual—a visit to Georgie's grave, which is located only a few yards from the graves of dozens of other human souls laid to rest in the adjoining cemetery. *Life and death in such close proximity*, Joni often notes, prompting worries about the quality of her groundwater. But the other day the cemetery brought to mind a recent conversation she'd had with a long-distance friend who phoned her out of the blue to tell her that she'd become a medium.

"A medium! That's so . . . different!" Joni exclaimed, recognizing the over-enthusiasm that creeps into her voice whenever she is trying to compensate for her dubiousness. (*You're fifty-six and trying to get pregnant? Good for you!*)

Joni's friend proceeded to share a wrenching story about how she had met the love of her life, but only a year later the man was struck by a car and killed.

Fucking cars, Joni thought.

"I needed to talk to him," her friend continued, "but I didn't know how, so I went to a medium who told me things that only my boyfriend and I could know. This medium helped me heal, but something else happened, as well."

"What? What else happened?" Joni felt a chill ripple up her spine.

"I realized I was really good at communicating with the dead," her friend shared. "From my first try, I dropped into a place that I didn't know existed and holy cow! I discovered that the greater reality is far more accessible than I ever imagined." She chuckled, then added, "So that's how I became a medium."

Joni marveled at this woman's resiliency, and at the human psyche's ability to manufacture coping mechanisms. "But what exactly does a medium do?" Joni asked, curious.

"You want to be in a state of active listening," her friend explained. "For example, I asked my boyfriend to define our relationship now that he's dead and he told me, 'We're in a *vibrationship*.'"

"A vibrationship?" Joni wanted to make sure that she'd heard correctly.

"Yes, a vibrationship," her friend repeated. "A meaningful connectivity between two people on different vibrational octaves."

At this last spot on the running route, Joni always blows Georgie a kiss. She would love to believe that her beloved pet is dodging clouds in heaven, and that all these dead neighbors are enjoying healthy vibrationships. Still, for Joni, the afterlife remains a black hole. Now though, thanks to her conversation with her friend the medium, she is more apt to linger between Georgie's grave and the neighboring cemetery, hoping to access a greater reality. So far, the silence that has greeted her tells her that she will probably never be able to communicate with the loved ones she has lost. Then again, Joni crosses her fingers, it never hurts to listen.

Queen Be

"Does anybody have any interesting news?"

This is the question I often ask at the start of each of my weekly writing classes, and while the implication is that I'm asking about *writing-related* insights, I'm secretly hoping for more titillating news, like the time one woman announced an ermine had moved into her house and let her rub its belly, or when three different participants in three back-to-back workshops had recently received the results of their DNA tests and learned their fathers weren't their fathers. These are the things happening in people's everyday worlds that make me shake my head in wonder.

But this particular week a novelist named April offered this: she'd just learned from a woman in her other writing group—that group focused more on finding a publisher rather than on narrative craft—that the latest taboo among agents and editors is the word *was.*

"Was?" I repeated. "You mean like the past tense of the verb *to be,* as in to live or exist?"

"Yep, *was.*" April confirmed. "One of the other members from that group had shared that an editor had expressed interest in her manuscript but would only consider acquiring it if the writer was willing to delete all the *wases.* Apparently, the word 'was' has become a real bugaboo among editors and agents."

But why this verb, I thought, instead of, say, the verb *squish,* which rarely connotes anything pleasant. Plus, in some cases the word *was* also falls into the category of an auxiliary verb, also known as a helping verb, that is used to express, among other things, passivity. Note the important distinction between the active and passive voice:

She threw herself into her kidnapper's trunk!

versus

She was thrown into her kidnapper's trunk!

Without the help of *was* to indicate passivity in that second sentence, people might think the protagonist actively wanted to be kidnapped, which would change her characterization dramatically and, frankly, make me stop caring about what's going to happen to someone so eager to please.

As it turned out, the week April shared the news about the publishing industry's ban on the word "was" coincided with the timing of Queen Elizabeth II's funeral. And while the two incidents may seem unrelated, in my mind they conflated into a reminder that there are a lot of imperious people out there. If only I had a mute button for all the bossypants who make pronouncements; people who use their "authority" to make other folks do questionable things, like when a classmate of mine, Glenn Applebaum, insisted I taste the spoonful of pink powder he waved in front of my face.

"It's just Kool-Aid, you dingleberry," he said. "You'll like it, I promise!"

An hour later, my furious mother (who, inexplicably, was madder at me than at Glenn Applebaum when I told her what happened) hauled me into the emergency room, where I was more scared than sick because it turns out what I'd actually darted the tip of my tongue into was a spoonful of chemical fertilizer. When I told the doctor I didn't actually think I swallowed any, he gave me some Ipecac and that was that. A few years later, Glenn Applebaum and his family moved away, and I lost track of him, but I wouldn't be surprised if he'd grown up and changed his name to Jim Jones.

In the ten days (though it felt like years) that it took to bury the queen, the headlines, even in the American press, wailed about the death of the ninety-six-year-old monarch as if we had lost our very own royal or favorite grandma. The whole concept of royalty is anathema to my proletarian senses. I find it ridiculous that just because some family centuries ago decided they were better than everyone else, now the rest of us have to act deferential and abide by bizzarro protocol, like how you can't turn your back to the queen when you leave the room, or how you're not allowed to keep eating once the queen has finished her meal.

"So, you're telling me I have to wait until my ass hits the door before I can turn around?" That is just one thing I've imagined saying if I ever got invited to Buckingham Palace. That and, *"No wonder this country is full of clotted cream."*

Still, despite my disrelish toward all things royal, I could not *not* read about the thousands of people queuing up for hours and hours to view the queen's casket, or get sucked down the rabbit hole of royal trivia: *The Queen prefers baths instead of showers . . . The Queen invented the "dorgi" when one of her beloved Corgis mated with Princess Margaret's dachshund . . . The Queen published her first Instagram post in 2019!* And then there were the countless times I found myself viewing that inescapable footage of Charles, heir to the throne, wiping away a tear at his mother's funeral. Call me an ugly American but swiping one tear does not erase the reality that the man is an entitled snob who actually has a valet tasked with putting exactly one inch of toothpaste on his toothbrush every morning.

Charles was seventy-three when he lost his mum (official cause of Her Majesty's death: old age), so you can't tell me that part of him wasn't thinking when he swiped that tear, *It's about bloody well time!* Meanwhile, I'm thinking, *How is someone fit to be king if he can't even squeeze a tube of toothpaste?*

As coverage of Queen Elizabeth's funeral consumed the headlines for days and days, I found myself longing for a return to normal, back when all I had to confront every morning was the usual onslaught of horrific headlines. But you know what they say—when one column inch closes another one opens. As soon as the queen was finally laid to rest in her vault, up popped headlines about an entirely different breed of (self-appointed) authority figures—the rising number of national and local groups on a tear to ban school libraries from including books on gender and race, as well as other topics they found offensive or controversial.

You have to admire their gall, these book banners. They show up at board meetings, some of them armed, telling school librarians which books did—or did not—belong on the shelves.

Banned! *Charlotte's Web* because talking animals are "unnatural and blasphemous."

Banned! *The Family Book* because it reveals the shocking reality that families come in all shapes, sizes, and colors.

Banned! The dictionary because the word "bed" is also defined as a verb.

Equally galling, many of these banners didn't even have kids in the schools and hadn't bothered to read any of the books they were rabidly protesting. I imagined what it must be like when these group members got together for their banning meetings. Probably not all that different from a book group I once belonged to, in which few, if any of us, had actually mustered the time or effort to read the chosen novel, so we just drank a lot of rosé and turned into mean drunks.

I think because I hang out with writers, and I'm someone who pretends to read much more widely than she actually does, I hear a lot of opinions about books, which has served to inure me to the authoritarian demands of both banners and bibliophiles alike:

"Joni, you simply must read Ayn Rand's Atlas Shrugged *about the morality of rational self-interest!"*

"No. No, I really don't need to read about that, thank you very much."

But that demonstration of independent thinking doesn't mean that I'm not susceptible to other types of imperatives and the sway of certain people who want to tell me what I can and cannot do. In fact, right around the time the rising number of book banners were grabbing headlines, another article appeared in my newsfeed written by a fellow named Adam, who was advocating for another kind of ban—*What Women over 50 Must NEVER Wear!*

No ripped jeans!

No Gap tees!

No fleece!

It was like Adam was reporting live from my closet. Also included on his list of banned clothing were Ugg boots, peasant blouses, choker necklaces, and magnifying mirrors, though I would place money on the fact that no woman over fifty has ever worn a magnifying mirror, unless maybe she perched one on her shoulder for an emergency pluck job, given you never know when your chin might sprout an unsightly hair.

It bothered me that Adam didn't just get inside my closet, but inside my head, making me second-guess a large swath of my wardrobe. *So you tell me,* I found myself arguing with Adam as I got dressed in the mornings, *how a thin-blooded woman, probably twice your age, is supposed to survive a Vermont winter without her Sherpa fleece hoodie?*

But was Adam really the problem? I thought. Likely he was just another struggling millennial, wishing that he was Adam *Lambert* the rock star instead of Adam the junior reporter, stuck writing articles that only exacerbated his mommy issues. Or maybe Adam actually believed what he was writing. (*Never wear cubic zirconia! You're an old woman, not a 16-year-old headed to the junior prom!*) Either way it was unsettling how I let him get to me and second guess myself.

I recalled another example of when I abandoned my better judgment while under the influence of a self-proclaimed authority figure. It happened in one of those situations where I think a lot of us are at our most susceptible, that is when we are sucked into one of those infomercials touting some amazing product, with a countdown clock running at the top of the screen, indicating we have only thirty-nine minutes and twenty-seven seconds left to save 50 percent on our first order! In this particular case, I was transfixed by a spokesmodel who was telling me how she had gone from bloated and lethargic to trim and full of energy, and now she was insisting that I do the same.

"Buy this miracle cleanse NOW!" she commanded. "It's like an internal shower!"

The spokesmodel's adamancy—along with my own desire to be trim and full of energy—explains why my kitchen cupboard now holds an oversized tub of a high-priced, stool-stimulating green powder that tastes like grass, or rather grass that had been sprayed with chemical fertilizer, and believe me I should know. (Thank you, Glenn Applebaum.) The minute I ordered the cleanse, I knew I didn't want it. Why did I allow this spokesmodel to override my own sanity? Why did I even think that my intestines needed cleaning? They're entrails for godsakes; they're supposed to be dirty.

"Does anybody have any interesting news?"

The last time I asked that question to my writing group, I thought about sharing my own news—how I had spent an inordinate number of hours going through an already clean manuscript, trying to stomp out all my *wases*. It had felt a bit like playing Whack-a-Mole on paper, a game that had always struck me as excessive and violent, especially given moles, like helping verbs, have many good qualities. Of course, I understood why agents and editors felt the need to caution writers about the verb *to be* and the passive voice. Indeed, the passive voice explained in a nutshell my antipathy toward royalty, given how the "subject" of the sentence is *acted upon* by some other performer of the verb. But a total ban on a verb meaning to live or exist? That made about as much sense as a dorgi.

Everywhere, it seemed, people were using whatever authority they claimed to impose arbitrary, extreme, or even absurd sets of rules on the rest of us. Equally disturbing was how easy it is to find your usually sensible head nodding along, even when another part of you is thinking, *really?* I'm reminded of how easy it is to be intimidated, sucked in, or briefly swayed every time I open my kitchen cupboard and see that big tub of disgusting green cleanse, which I can't throw away because it costs too much money.

But back to my writing group. I didn't, but I should have, told the others in the group about my recent afternoon spent trying to stomp out all my *wases*. I think I was embarrassed to admit how readily I had abandoned my own editorial instincts—culled from twenty-plus years of teaching—and succumbed to the authority of those agents and editors. If I were a queen, I thought (and, despite my dislike of royalty, the idea greatly appealed), I would make a few proclamations of my own.

First, I would ban all the banners (except for me of course, which shows just how easy it is to let authority go to your head).

Second, I would encourage everyone of every age to wear more fleece because when I do, I just feel comfier.

And third, I would start a campaign to save the verb *was*, because sometimes people should just let other people *to be*.

120 Seconds

A Too-Short Movie

FADE IN:

EXT. TRAFFIC INTERSECTION, SMALL TOWN, VERMONT—6:00 P.M.

JONI, middle-aged, nondescript. As she approaches the traffic light ahead it turns yellow. She brakes and waits at the light.

CUT TO:

INT. JONI'S TOYOTA

Her purse and a bag of groceries rest on the passenger seat.

JONI

(VO of her thoughts)

What did she read somewhere? A typical red light
lasts 120 seconds.

She looks out the window, watches the cars. It's the usual amount of small-town traffic, people heading home from work. She starts counting in her head, a habit when she's killing time.

JONI

(VO of her thoughts)

One . . . two . . . three . . . four . . . five . . .

Her thoughts drift to TOM, age twenty-two, her daughter's friend. The one time she met him, Tom and her daughter sat close on the couch. Clearly, the two of them were smitten. He struck her as a nice young man, smart, well-spoken. As is often the case when Joni is waiting at a light, the following scene plays in her mind:

DISSOLVE TO:

EXT. TRAFFIC INTERSECTION, NORTHEAST WASHINGTON, DC, 6:00 P.M.

TOM, aspiring social worker, lanky, good-looking, sporting a man-bun. He's driving home to the house he shares with fellow volunteers at a nonprofit that helps recovering addicts find jobs. The traffic light ahead turns yellow. He brakes and waits at the light.

CUT TO:

INT. TOM'S JEEP

An open backpack rests on the passenger seat. Tom's gym bag and muddy hiking boots are tossed in the back. He glances at the file poking out of the backpack.

TOM

(VO of his thoughts)

Note to self. Make sure to text Antonio, reminding
him he's got that second interview tomorrow with
the manager at the car detailing shop. God, I hope
he stays clean. At least his two sons are speaking to
him again.

Tom leans over, rummages in the messy glove compartment, pulls out a
granola bar, eats it. Crumbs fall on his lap.

TOM

(VO of his thoughts)

Damn. Someone's gonna condemn this car if I don't
clean it up pretty soon.

Tom looks out the window, watches the usual flow of rush-hour city
traffic, drums on the steering wheel.

TOM

(VO of his thoughts)

Glad my commute's only five minutes. Man, I'm
starving. Wonder who's cooking tonight? Maybe
it's the new guy at the house. He seems pretty cool.
I should ask if he wants to go hiking with us this
weekend.

Tom rubs his neck, stiff from a long day of meetings, phone calls, a tough
conversation with a client who didn't show up at his job.

TOM

(VO of his thoughts)

What a weird couple months. Harder than I thought,
but it's feeling like the right choice, to stick with
social work. I should get going on those grad school
applications.

Tom speed-dials his dad's number, puts the call on speaker. It goes
straight to voicemail.

TOM

(leaving message)

Hey, Dad. Sorry I missed you. Anyway, everything's
cool here. Job's good. I've finally decided to go ahead
with grad school. We can talk about it some more
when I see you in a couple weeks. I could use some
of your cooking. Anyway, I m just heading back to
the house from work. I'll try you later. Tell Mom hi,
and not to worry. Everything's good.

Tom disconnects the call, glances at the gas gauge.

TOM

(VO of his thoughts)

I better hit the Shell station in Bladensburg. Nah. I
don't want to be late for dinner. I'll fill up this weekend before we head out to the trail.

Tom glances out the window. He notices a few guys hanging out in front
of one of the rowhouses across the intersection.

TOM

(VO of his thoughts)

Maybe if I stay in DC, I'll look into getting an apartment around here, in Trinidad. It's pretty safe, at
least not any worse than a lot of other areas in the
city. Thank God this job comes with free housing.
I'm lucky how things worked out.

Tom goes back to staring at the light. He starts counting in his head, a
habit when he's killing time.

TOM

(VO of his thoughts)

One . . . two—man I'm hungry—three . . . four . . . five . . .

A shot rings out. Tom's body slumps forward. He's bleeding from his
head.

TOM

(VO of his thoughts)

. . . six . . . seven . . .

The light turns green. Tom is dead.

DISSOLVE TO:

INT. JONI'S CAR—6:02 P.M.

JONI

(VO of her thoughts)

. . . six . . . seven . . .

Joni remains seated in her car, her face tight with emotion. She shakes her head, trying to erase the scene lingering in her mind.

JONI

(VO of her thoughts)

He was twenty-two years old. Just sitting at a
light. One-hundred-and-twenty seconds. If only
that light had changed just a few seconds sooner.
Everything would have been different. Tom would
still be alive.

A horn sounds. She realizes the traffic light has turned green. She drives forward.

JONI

(VO of her thoughts)

That man bun . . .

Joni smiles at the memory of Tom sitting next to her daughter on the couch, their knees touching.

JONI

(VO of her thoughts)

He almost pulled it off. But then again, a nice young

guy like Tom—smart, well-spoken, clearly smitten—
he could have done almost anything.

FADE TO BLACK:

A postscript appears on screen:

Tom M. was the 135th homicide victim of the year in Washington, DC, far surpassing last year's total of 116.

END

〰

Will Work For . . .

"Are you going to be okay?" The question comes from the chatty silver-haired lady at the front table of the Tax-Aide office. She is not the one who will be preparing my taxes, but rather the intake volunteer assigned to organize my paperwork for Chuck, my regular tax guy. This intake process is a new and disturbing feature of Tax-Aide. For the past several years I have simply handed everything to the discreet and capable Chuck, then slunk away, and somehow my taxes got e-filed. In short, Chuck treated me exactly the way I want to be treated in this situation—as little more than a faceless Tax ID number.

But not this concerned volunteer. For the past several minutes, she has held me hostage with her questions and commentary, as she rummages through my messy pile of 1099s, hand-scrawled expenses, and likely the results of my last colonoscopy, because whenever I am doing or thinking about anything even remotely related to taxes, I get anxious and slapdash.

Are you going to be okay? What exactly does this woman mean by *okay*? Does she think I am physically ill? No doubt, my features are puckered tighter than a jewelry pouch, but this is my resting tax face. Plus, she is taking forever. (*"Hmm. Does Chuck like the 1099MISCs to be filed before or after the 1099R? Now, this is interesting! A Form 8829!"*) I have neither the stomach nor time for this kind of fastidiousness. This was supposed to be a quick drop off. In exactly forty-five minutes I have to be back in my home office to teach an online writing workshop.

"What do you mean by okay?" I make myself ask, though already I assume she is thinking the worst:

You owe a billion dollars . . .

You are going to be arrested for tax fraud . . .

I know who you are and I saw what you did.

This last line is from a movie I watched years ago, in which two teenage girls are making prank calls and just happen to phone a man who had murdered his wife that very day and disposed of her body in the woods. All paranoia aside, this intake volunteer actually does know who I am and what I have done, as evidenced by her friendly greeting when I arrived at the front table. "I went to your talk at the library awhile back," she'd said, offering me a smile. "Are you working on another book?"

Normally, I enjoy this kind of small-town sociability. Indeed, I particularly like the little thrill of importance that comes when someone whom I don't recognize clearly recognizes me. But, in this case, the woman's familiarity only adds to my anxiety because, when it comes to my personal finances, I don't want anybody—especially anybody who goes to the same library as me—knowing where I've buried the bodies.

"This is bad news . . ." The intake volunteer—Sheila according to her name tag—holds up one of my documents, a 1098T showing the educational expenses related to my younger daughter's last year of college. Her expression is grim, like she's just seen a dark shadow on an X-ray. "You're not going to be able to claim your graduate as a dependent next year," she explains. "That's really going to hurt your situation."

Next year? She's talking about my situation next year? Oh, for the love of God! I can't think about next year. I'm too consumed with anxiety about this tax season. And why wouldn't I be? Everyone knows, it's never the fat cats who get harassed by the IRS. It's always the little guys, the ones living paycheck to paycheck, the drug dealers, the prostitutes, the mid-list authors and writing workshop instructors who get called out for not reporting every cent of their income. I am neither a drug dealer nor a prostitute, but I am self-employed, which is basically the same thing to the IRS, which expects all of us to report every cent of our earnings—legal or otherwise— on Schedule C.

"So this 1099-NEC," Sheila holds up another form, pointing to the small figure on line 1. "Is this the total amount of your royalties?" I nod pleasantly, acting like this kind of public humiliation is fun for me. I'm sorry I'm not Jodi Picoult, I think, for more reasons than one. Jodi Picoult is not only one of the world's most successful authors, she also happens to live only minutes away from me, but you can bet your ass she doesn't get her taxes done at Tax-Aide, a freebie service offered by AARP.

Sheila continues examining my forms, keeping up a running commentary, as much for her own benefit as mine. To my ear, it sounds like she could be dictating my financial autopsy report—"White woman, middle-aged, no sign of suffering past trauma such as systemic poverty, environmental disaster, health crisis, or crippling divorce. Disproportionately low income levels suggest cause of death due to pre-existing condition as an English major, exacerbated by an intolerance for working a 'real job' plus weakened fourth quarter sales figures of her latest book . . ."

My foot starts tapping. I check my phone, then glance around the room at the scattering of tables, most of them occupied by elderly people. I noticed this phenomenon last year, as well, that hardly anyone on the younger side of fifty and up seems to take advantage of this AARP service, maybe because they have too much pride, or money, or don't share my fear and loathing of Turbo Tax.

A woman, maybe in her eighties, wearing a mustard-colored sweater, arrives and waits her turn in one of the plastic chairs by the entrance. The mustard, in combination with the fluorescent lighting, casts a ghoulish shadow on her pallor. Seeing this elderly woman by the door, clutching her slim pile of paperwork, is when it hits me, the real cause of Sheila's concern. My kindly intake volunteer isn't simply worried about the state of my finances next year, when I can no longer mooch tax benefits from my daughter. What she is really worried about is my situation in the foreseeable future. *Sure, this author from the library has managed to make ends meet up to now,* Sheila is likely thinking, *but what happens when she is that old woman in the mustard sweater? What's going to become of her when she is ghoulish and is no longer able to work?*

Retirement. I've heard of it, of course. It's what people do when they have enough money to leave their jobs. I have several retired friends, some older, some younger, but most of them seem to have mastered the concept. They volunteer; they take safaris; they spend quality time with their grandkids; they rekindle their creative sides; they look ridiculous, but happy, on their recumbent bikes. Several of my retired friends live in fancy houses. A few of them, I worry, might be struggling financially or emotionally, but most are living the cliché—"I've never been busier than after I retired."

But, even if I could afford to retire, which one glance at form 1099-NEC suggests otherwise, what would that look like for someone like me; someone who works from home. Right now, my office is my daughter's bedroom, which I took over when she moved to California, though ownership reverts back to her when she comes home for visits. But retirees don't go into the office, and if they do it can look a bit pathetic among a sea of fresh faces—"Oh, there's old Jack, hanging out by the water cooler. I heard he was the top sales guy back in the seventies." This image begs the question: If I retired, should I stay out of my daughter's bedroom? That certainly was her preference when she was in high school, but what about when she returns to visit her old mom, and I feel the urge to kiss my long-lost deduction goodnight?

The truth is, I actually like that my office is in my daughter's bedroom. The room is painted turquoise and gets lots of light. The bed is covered with my manuscripts and teaching materials, guarded by my cat and by Ted, my daughter's favorite stuffed animal from childhood. When I need a change of pace from this room, I work downstairs in the kitchen, or I write from the living room couch. Basically, much of my workday involves shuffling around my condo, rarely leaving the house, but that's okay because I am very much a homebody. The thought occurs that, if I retired, I probably still wouldn't go much of anywhere, but then I wouldn't get paid for staying at home.

"Is this a seven or a nine?" Sheila intrudes on my thoughts, pointing to a squiggle on my illegible list of itemized expenses.

"Nine," I say, though it's just as likely a seven. I hope I have guessed in a tax-advantageous direction. I shuffle in my chair, then stop shuffling because I read somewhere that shuffling is a "tell." The last thing I need is for Sheila to catch on to the fact that almost all of these numbers are guesstimates, determined less by receipts and more by my third eye chakra, that sixth sense telling me that I'd better find me some write-offs. Regardless of my impatience and tight timeframe, I do appreciate Sheila's attention to detail, especially when I recall my experience with the bookkeeper at my first full time job in advertising way back when. Day one, the woman plopped a bunch of payroll forms on my desk to complete, then abandoned me to make sense of them on my own. The next tax year, I ended up owing the IRS nine thousand dollars, and this on a junior copywriter's salary!*

Thinking about that job reminds me how much I disliked it; how miserable and ill-suited I felt as an employee in all the regular jobs I'd had from my twenties to forties. Even if the work held some appeal, even when I liked my coworkers or clients, I hated the confinement of a nine-to-five schedule; I hated having a boss, even a nice boss, telling me what to do and when to do it. But, of course, self-employment comes with its own set of challenges. For instance, most of the bosses I had before I became self-employed were a whole lot easier to work for than me. Also, when I am under deadline for one or all of the jobs I have cobbled together as an author, teacher, and freelance extra-income chaser, my time is hardly my own.

"You're always working," my older daughter said to me just a few Saturdays ago, as I was hunched on the couch, typing away under pressure. Her voice held no resentment, but her words gave me a pang, remembering how both my girls have said the same thing to me before, when they were little, then teenagers, and now as young adults. But even if I could quit working, even if money was no longer a factor, then what? Like so many others, I have fantasized about winning the Powerball jackpot, except my fantasy always ends with me in the same boat as those other winners who quit their jobs, then quickly squander all their winnings and wind up miserable. This is the so-called curse of the lottery, a phenomenon aptly named, and there is no doubt in my mind that this curse would befall me. I think I'd be adrift if I wasn't teaching and writing because my work gives me purpose; it fulfills me. Plus, I don't have any hobbies.

---

* About that nine thousand dollars I owed to the IRS on my junior copywriter salary. It turns out I'd listed my four housemates as dependents, though you would have thought the bookkeeper at the ad agency would have caught my error, given I was twenty-six and single at the time. Did she really think I'd already given birth to four children?

Recently, I was complaining to a friend about too many deadlines and how stressed I was feeling.

"Take a break," he advised. "Don't do anything this weekend."

"But if I'm not doing anything," I asked, "then what would I do?"

Finally, Sheila completes the challenge of putting my forms in order and deciphering my penmanship. She tucks the tidy package of my last fiscal year into a Tax-Aide folder. "You're good to go, at least for now," she tells me, rapping a knuckle three times on the folder. I thank her and hurry toward the exit, passing the elderly woman with the ghoulish mustard pallor. The ghost of tax seasons yet to come, I think.

The clock on my car's dash allows me eighteen minutes to arrive home for my class, but I hear time ticking down in more ways than one.

At home, the first of the day's two creative writing workshops goes well; its participants are a talented and appreciative bunch. I, on the other hand, am not my usual attentive self, distracted by a leftover unease from the morning's visit to the Tax-Aide office. It occurred to me during the workshop that, sure, I am in demand now as a teacher, but what happens if—or rather when—people stop wanting to take my classes? What happens when I become poor retired Jack, hanging out at the water cooler, with no one for company except Ted, the stuffed bear, who also knows what it feels like to outlast your usefulness.

Downstairs, I eat some lunch at the kitchen counter and contemplate the reasoning—or lack of—related to my professional life choices. If only being an employee and having a regular job wasn't anathema to me, I think. If only I'd done what all those financial advisors recommend for a "comfortable retirement," which is basically to open an IRA when you're old enough to start babysitting. And on top of this, Sheila's question—*Are you going to be okay?*—has put an ironic twist on my situation, given that sometime in my retirement years, a regular job may be exactly where I'm heading. Just recently I saw an ad with the heading: *Earn Extra Cash in Retirement!* At the time, it wasn't the message that drew my attention, but the image of a senior, squatting to stock a lower food shelf. Really, I thought. Is that the kind of job appropriate for someone with knee replacements? But now the thought of that ad raises a different concern. I imagine myself, five, ten. maybe thirty years from now, my face in folds, my body stooped. I am standing at the main intersection of my little town, holding up a square of cardboard with a message scrawled in my illegible handwriting: "WILL WORK . . . FOREVER!"

By now, all this tax nonsense, and thinking about the money I don't have and never will have has left me confronting a question that has become more pressing with each passing year: Did I make the right choice to do what I do; to quit that last full-time job two decades ago and never reconsider? The answer is writ large on Form 8829, and my scrawled attempt to rustle up some expenses for the business use of my home. Despite Sheila's efforts, it is obvious that no amount of knocking three times on my tax file is likely to bring enough good fortune to make up for a nest egg equivalent in size to that of a bee hummingbird's. Yet, even as my retirement age gets pushed back to never, I still can't manage any regrets. For too many years than I care to remember, I'd wake up dreading the workday, and that wasn't a tradeoff I was willing to make.

After lunch, I head upstairs to my sunny, turquoise office, planning to put in a few hours. Instead, I shift some piles of paper to the edge of the bed and remove Ted from the pillow. Despite afternoon deadlines— always more deadlines—I am tired and curl up for a nap. This is yet another reason I love being self-employed. I can sleep on the job, and even my bossypants boss can't fault me because we both know that if I'm going to work forever, I'd better rest up while I can.

One Day at a Time

My name is Joni, and I am a recovering program director.

It all started when the board of a boutique literary festival asked me if I would be interested in designing a program of author readings for its upcoming three-day event. Founded a decade ago, the festival had been on hiatus for two years, but now the board was hoping to bring it back bigger and better than ever!

"You're an author, a writing teacher, a podcaster!" the board chairman gushed, or at least it sounded like gushing to me. "Please tell us you'll take the job!"

Naturally, I was flattered because, hey, a little recognition for what I'd been doing forever felt long overdue. Already, I could imagine curating diverse literary luminaries and crosscultural voices. The majority of them, of course, would be the usual suspects, but with the power invested in me I could help a few no-names rise from obscurity. I could show some respect to those mid-list authors like me, whose publishers stopped taking their calls just because they no longer held the promise of a fresh-faced debut. I could dole out favors to my author friends, a demonstration of my omnibenevolence and superiority.

"Yes," I replied, fingers twitching in anticipation. "I humbly accept the job of program director." My God, I thought, my very own literary festival! Just that word—*literary*—implicative of learnedness, quality of form, elitism! I would elevate this small-town festival to a status equal to the popular Brooklyn Book Festival, the massive Frankfurt Book Fair, or even SleuthFest that blatantly caters to all those obsessive fans of mystery and suspense.

As I left the meeting, I felt an unfamiliar surge of self-importance. Even my unfinished manuscript I always lugged around with me in my shoulder bag felt more literary, more worthy of publication. Looking back now, I think I sensed from the very beginning that the job held a dangerous allure. *I can handle it,* I told myself. *I can quit anytime.* But, in the end, being the program director of a boutique literary festival almost cost me everything.

Week one. News traveled fast, and queries from eager authors started appearing in my inbox. In years past, I was always the one imploring some other program director to allow me to do a reading at their bookstore, or library, or conference; to allow me a seat on the publishing panel; to invite me to be "in conversation with" somebody, anybody. But now! Oh, how quickly the tables had turned:

> Dear Ms. Cole, I am writing to nominate myself and another Vermont poet for participation in your literary festival . . .

> Dear Joni, the *New York Times* described my new best-selling memoir as a gripping story . . .

> Dear program director, I hope this email finds you well! I am an award-winning novelist who would love to share my latest work with your audience . . .

Because this boutique festival could only accommodate forty author events (not like those bigger festivals willing to let in all sorts of emerging authors) I knew I would need to be thoughtful and judicious in how I selected my presenters.

No!

No!

No!

Those first three queries were instant hard passes. I rejected the two Vermont poets because I had never heard of them, and Vermont is not all that big! As for the memoirist with the "gripping story," I just had a *feeling* she was full of herself. And that person who would love to share his latest work with my audience? Why would I include him when he couldn't even be bothered to learn my name!

As the days passed, I continued to dole out noes and the occasional yes like the whims of a despot. No, to the novelist whose name reminded me of someone I hated in middle school. Yes, to the author who wished me a happy birthday on Facebook. No, to a slew of poets with their little chapbooks. (Did they really think their slim volumes—with half the pages nothing but white space—earned them a podium at my festival?) And no, no, a thousand times no to my long-time nemesis, a chipper woman from my former writing group who went on to publish three best sellers of upmarket fiction, and lives on a picturesque alpaca farm. (Technically speaking, this woman never queried me about presenting at the festival, but I still got a thrill just fantasizing about sending her a rejection.)

Of course, even as I was weeding out the riff raff, I also was extending invitations, such as one to my favorite novelist Audrey T., a woman of belles lettres. "I'd be delighted," she wrote back almost immediately. In appreciation for her promptness, I followed up by sending Audrey T. my unfinished manuscript. It was shortly after this exchange that I made the decision to capitalize "Program Director" on all my correspondence, and began referring to myself in the third person.

> The Program Director has a particular disdain for confessional memoirs . . .

> The Program Director is willing to consider your application, pending receipt of your last three royalty statements.

> The Program Director requires that you submit an 85-word bio and high resolution headshot, and do not make her ask twice.

In hindsight, I can see that referring to myself in the third person should have been a big warning sign, but the rush of autocracy had clouded my judgment. Yes, I was aware of the adage—absolute power corrupts absolutely—but surely that was a problem for lower-case program directors, not for someone like me, capable of getting even Pulitzer-Prize winners and recipients of the National Book Award to bend to her will. Just look at how some of these luminaries responded to my recruiting efforts:

"Okay, okay. I've always enjoyed presenting at your festival in the past. The previous program director was such a lovely person."

"Well, I suppose I could skip my family reunion . . ."

"Alright already, I'll be your keynoter, but do you think you could possibly cover my air fare?"

That last author had to be kidding. What did I look like, Deutsche Bank?

In the past, I would have been starstruck or intimidated by these successful authors, but the Program Director had quickly learned that even the best sellers and prize winners still had to keep hawking the merchandise. Plus, unlike *real* celebrities, nobody ever remembers the names of authors. (*"Have you read that guy, you know, that guy who wrote a book about his lousy childhood, and they made it into a movie starring Benedict Cumberbatch?"*) Can anybody name me the winner of a single writing award, any writing award? How about the last recipient of the Booker Prize? The National Book Critics Circle Award? The Penn/Faulkner? The Newbery Medal? The Pushcart? The Caldecott? The O. Henry Prize? The Nebula Award? How about the friggin' Nobel Prize in Literature?

Anybody? Anybody? I didn't think so.

As the festival neared, I was riding high, on the cusp of creating the perfect program in my image, though I can't deny there were trouble spots along the way. I was *not* pleased when the author of a Reese's Book Club Pick got all pissy after I demanded she give me Reese's cell number. Several presenters balked at the non-disclosure agreement. And one touchy author raised quite the stink when I refused to correct the misspelling of her first name, but, really, who puts a "y" in Ellen. At this point, it was too late to blacklist these troublemakers, but I had my ways of keeping them in line. (*"You think just because Showtime based a series on your life story that you're entitled to a bottled water? Well, enjoy it during your event . . . that I just moved to Sunday at 6:30 a.m.!"*)

Still, I had no idea how bad things had become until the board of the literary festival—the same board members who had sought me out and gushed about my talents—summoned me to an emergency meeting. The subject line of the agenda read: *Intervention.*

"There have been multiple complaints," the chairman announced. "Several authors feel you're a terrible person."

From that point forward, it was a downward spiral. Audrey T. emailed me to cancel her participation, claiming she'd broken her leg in three places. (The nerve! Plus, she still hasn't thanked me for sending her my manuscript!) I got into a Twitter feud with the program director of SleuthFest. The local librarian filed a restraining order against me, claiming destruction of property just because I'd knocked down some dusty stacks to make space for my grand entrance. And I may have spray painted "AUDREY T. IS A SLUT!" on the front window of the town's quaint bookstore that had agreed to host the author signings.

But it wasn't until I ran into my nemesis at the bakery that sold my favorite cherry scones that I would say I officially hit rock bottom. She was in front of me in line, wearing another one of her hand-crafted alpaca sweaters.

"I was so happy when I heard you were the new program director," she said, chipper as always. "The board had asked me if I wanted the job, but I'm about to go on book tour, so I had to tell them no." She pointed to the last cherry scone in the case, requesting it, "to go."

I don't remember what happened next; I only know what played on the local news. The clip showed me tackling my nemesis, wrestling with her on the ground, grabbing fistfuls of alpaca. Oh, how I detested Huacaya fiber!

"The Program Director wanted that cherry scone!" I yelled at her, snatching the to-go bag from her fist. Why did this woman get everything I wanted? "That was supposed to be the Program Director's scone!"

After my nemesis ran off, calling for help (for once, thank God, not sounding so chipper), I lay on the floor, skirt askew, surrounded by the scattered pages of my unfinished manuscript that had fallen out of my shoulder bag. "Just once," I muttered, stuffing my face with cherry scone, "the Program Director wanted to be asked first."

Today marks six weeks since I last talked about myself in the third person. I have been working hard, trying to move forward with my life, and to not think about how that news footage of the bakery incident went viral on YouTube. (1.9 million views and counting. Oh my.) I am trying to make amends to the people whom I harmed, though I've been DMing like crazy and no one is messaging me back.

Of course, my time spent in lockdown meant that I couldn't attend the literary festival, but I would have missed it anyway, given that I'm legally prohibited to get within one-hundred yards of the library. But these past weeks have also given me time to reflect on my behavior, and to better understand what drove me to the brink.

When I was the Program Director, I felt important in ways that I had never experienced as a writer. The job served to numb the pain of so many years of anonymity and rejection. It overrode my insecurity around more successful, prize-winning authors who get invited to do readings without having to ask, who can live off their royalties, who get sent on book tours. It helped soothe the sting of those myriad paper cuts I'd always pretended to laugh off—all the empty seats at my author events; the friends and writing students who never offered even a quick congrats on a new release; and the one time I actually was invited to give a keynote address, only to have the person who introduced me mangle my name. As the Program Director, I got to be the one mangling another author's name, and it felt good. Really good.

Sometimes I ask myself, Why did I want my own literary festival? Was it simply for the power and prestige? I'm not going to lie, that's *exactly* why I took that job. The Program Director really wanted that cherry scone.

But are those the same reasons I wanted to be a writer?

No.

Maybe.

No!

If you're a writer, I am learning, it's the work that matters, not being a best selling author or winning an award. You don't choose to be a writer to impress your friends and fellow authors and students, and you certainly don't do it for the money. The writing itself is the reward. At least that's what I'm going to keep telling myself, one day at a time.

Save the Date

Dennis Rodman did it, so why can't I? The admittedly eccentric basket-ball player married himself, arriving for the ceremony in a horse-drawn carriage, wearing a custom French wedding dress, and attended by a wedding party of women in tuxedos. Dennis Rodman's self-marriage might have been a publicity stunt to sell his new book (note to self—would that work for me?!), but for several years I, too, have seriously toyed with this notion of sologamy. Though that word—which I hear as *slog*-amy—makes it sound like a lot of work, and if that's what it's like being married to me, well, my ex-husband probably wouldn't argue.

And yet.

I love weddings. Mine and everyone else's, which takes me by sur-prise. My own wedding some thirty years ago was a slapdash fifteen-person affair set at a colonial tavern in Paradise, Pennsylvania, in Amish Country, just a few miles down the road from towns called Blue Ball, Bird-in-Hand, and Intercourse. Having grown up near these commu-nities, not to mention the fact that I am an adult, these town names shouldn't make me titter, but, seriously, look at their tourist brochures: *Worship at the Blue Ball Mennonite Church . . . Fun Things to Do in Intercourse!*

It was three weeks tops from the engagement to the wedding, and one week of that time was spent apart from my soon-to-be-husband, Steve, because he was hundreds of miles away in graduate school. The January rain on my wedding day was bad for my permed hair, but a sign of good luck because, according to superstition, if it's raining when you "tie the knot" your marriage is harder to unravel.

The particulars of my big day were no fuss—we arranged for a ceremony set at a pretty, historical inn, performed by a chaplain borrowed from a local hospital. I had never been that person who planned her wedding since childhood. I prefer practical to romantic—maybe to a fault? For both me and Steve, the long-distance nature of our relationship—should we split up or commit?—was getting old. The wedding would force-stop our indecisiveness, or, as my wise mother told me when I asked her advice, "Either shit or get off the pot."

That mentality might have been what motivated the marriage, but the wedding itself transcended practicality, or even romance, in ways I never could have anticipated. I knew some people see the formality of marriage as simply a piece of paper, and I might have been one of them, until I felt the power of the act. In the ritual of exchanging vows, in the promise to have and to hold, I had what can only be described as a spiritual experience, a term I don't use lightly because when other people start tossing it around, I tend to look for the exits.

Even now, decades later and divorced, memories of my wedding ceremony take me to that sacred space. Even when I attend other people's weddings, the everyday world recedes, as I witness the exchange of vows. During those moments, there is no room for statistics, like the fact that 45 percent of marriages end in divorce. It doesn't matter that two weeks earlier the bride and maid of honor were fighting over shoe dye. Who cares if the relationship started with an affair? Marriage is not just a piece of paper. It sanctifies commitment, love, even grace.

I have floated this idea of marrying myself by my two daughters, some friends, even my boyfriend, Helmut.

"It's a real thing," I reassure them. "You can read all about sologamy in *Brides* magazine, and people talk about it on mindfulness podcasts."

"Are you serious?" they ask, and I understand their confusion. For one thing, I'm not the type of person who gravitates toward this kind of behavior, meaning the kind of behavior that could land you a guest spot in that third hour of the *Today Show* in that segment called: "Older women who still do adorable-slash-outlandish things." Yet, the concept of making a commitment to yourself continues to intrigue me, especially given how so many people, myself included, spend an inordinate amount of time live-tweeting their faults and inadequacies between their own ears.

Usually I am a decisive person, the opposite of a vacillator. *I want this . . . I hate that. I'm going . . . I'm not going and you can't make me.* For me, even a rash decision is far more palatable than the limbo of uncertainty and the drag of emotional energy left in its wake. On the subject of self-marriage, however, this is an idea I have been toying with for at least three peak wedding seasons. *Do it . . . Don't be silly . . . Do it . . .* What could be the downside?

Sologamy. Self-love. Self-care. Each a holograph of the other, but it's that last term—*self-care*—that makes me wince. Do I want to jump on that bandwagon, that self-care gravy train that, to my ear, has become one of the most obnoxious marketing buzzwords on the planet? During the civil rights era, the term self-care represented a radical concept translated into a movement to assure underserved people had the time, money, and resources to this basic human right—the right to care for themselves. In the words of the late activist Audre Lorde, "self-care is not self-indulgence, it is self-preservation."

Today though, I imagine Audre Lorde herself needing a luxury getaway under a weighted blanket infused with essential oils just to recover from the way companies and advertisers have co-opted the term to sell overpriced products, and how the opposite of the underserved use the self-care movement as an excuse to pamper the bejesus out of themselves. *"Self-care is a basic human right . . . so I'm going to Ibiza for the month."*

I worry, is my inclination toward an event where I am the center of attention just an excuse for this kind of indulgence? In Googling the word "sologamy," one of the first listings I came across was a four-day solo-wedding package (inclusive with limo, photography, flowers, and a shaman!) at a "breathtaking" all-suite resort. The photos showed a goddess-type model standing in a stone circle, surrounded by her goddess-like attendants, all of which made me think, *Those are exactly the kind of people I'm not inviting to my wedding.*

In my work as a creative writing teacher, when writers feel stuck because they don't know what should happen next, I often suggest they stop overthinking, and simply start writing their way to clarity. *Just ask yourself: What if...? What if your character did this... or that? Play out the situation on the page. Follow your character. Let her show you what she wants to do.*

With this advice in mind, I decide to write my own what-if scenario, to play out the possibilities of my sologamy story. What if I did decide to marry myself? What would that look like? Will I actually show up for my nuptials, or leave myself stranded at the altar?

Setting. The first thing I commit to the page is an easy decision. I will get married right here in Vermont, my home state, and one of the premier locations for a destination wedding. I also like Vermont's open-minded attitude toward relationships, as evidenced by the fact that it was the first state to recognize civil unions back in the day. Love is love, or some iteration of this sentiment can be seen on countless Vermont lawn signs and bumper stickers, or at least the ones I choose to read. So, Vermont it is, with the actual location to be determined, though I do know wherever it takes place there will be lots and lots of twinkle lights.

The dress. Not white, but not because of that silly nonsense about second weddings, rather because of its unfortunate effect on my skin's yellow undertones. I suppose the age-appropriate thing would be to wear some kind of elegant suit, maybe something satiny or embellished with beads, but no. That's way too mother-of-the-bride for my taste, and I don't want to look like I'm my own mother at my wedding. I'll opt for a pretty pink dress and fun shoes with chunky heels!

The "giveaway." There will be no walking down any aisles, and not just because this custom stems from the days of arranged marriages, where the father's presence served as a reminder to the groom that he'd better not back out. I would feel too self-conscious, with all that rubbernecking when the bride enters the room, especially if there are any rubberneckers like me, who can't help thinking things like, *Oh, honey! You should have blended that foundation into your sweetheart neckline.*

The ring. Not a priority. I'm no fan of diamonds and while I'm partial to a plain wedding band, I could just use the one I already have in my keepsake drawer, yet another example of my preference for practical over romantic—maybe to a fault?

The vows. As an author by trade, it should be easy to write my own vows, but this is the part of my self-assigned creative writing exercise where I find myself blocked, totally blocked. Maybe, I wonder, it's because the vows are the whole point of this crazy notion of marrying myself. This is where the idea of sologamy goes from an excuse for a party to the heart of the matter—a declaration of self-love. *Don't overthink it,* I tell myself, and decide to simply tailor the traditional wedding vows to my occasion, typing them in a pretty script . . .

I, Joni, take myself to be my partner in life.

I imagine addressing these words to the woman in the pink dress—me—standing beneath a canopy of twinkle lights. It's funny, the tricks of the mind because, in this imagined scenario, I look different than the way I usually see myself. It's as if I am gazing at myself from the outside in; the way someone who is about to marry me would see me, through a tender heart.

To have and to hold from this day forward, for better, for worse, for richer, for poorer, in sickness and in health . . .

I look into my eyes, but not in the way I typically hone in on the lines and weariness creeping in at the corners. The lines around these blue eyes tell the story of a woman who has worked hard and could use a little more sleep. She laughs a lot, sometimes inappropriately, and stays up too late reading. She's spent a lot of time squinting into the sun. One of these days, I think, I'll manage to convince her to wear sunglasses.

To love and to cherish, till death us do part. This, I promise, is my solemn vow.

I start to cry, the way I always do at weddings. Just writing these words, I am moved by the power of these simple, traditional vows—a solemn commitment to love and to care for another person for the rest of their life. What could be more profound than two people exchanging this sacred promise at their wedding ceremony?

But two people aren't in this ceremony, I remind myself. It would just be me, exchanging vows with myself. I expect to think it silly, imagining myself standing all by my lonesome under a bunch of twinkle lights, but instead I feel . . . what? A surprising sadness. Why haven't I always loved and cherished myself? Why have I spent so much time focused on my faults and failings, too often feeling bad about this person who is fundamentally good? Why haven't I viewed myself through a tender heart?

I revisit the wedding vows typed on the page, but this time I read them aloud:

"I, Joni, take myself to be my partner in life. To have and to hold from this day forward . . . To love and to cherish, till death us do part."

That final line—"till death us do part"—comes with a significance impossible to ignore now that I am a good deal older than the last time I spoke these vows. I am so lucky not to be lacking in love from my children, my boyfriend, and close friends. I even feel love still exists between my ex-husband and myself, just not in the same way as when we were happily married. Still, life and time are relentless. Couples divorce. Friends come and go. The people you took for granted would be around forever leave or up and die on you, faster and faster it seems, with each passing season. So really, it strikes me, the only way you can be sure you are loved till the very end of your life, is if you make this commitment to yourself.

"This, I promise, is my solemn vow."

I know that I am alone at my desk, and have spoken these lines aloud for no one but myself to hear. But this little "what-if" ceremony I have just played out feels as real as reality, and nothing at all like self-care, or at least self-care as defined by a luxury getaway. If marriage is just a piece of paper, then this piece of paper where I have written my sologamy vows seems to prove once again that, for me, getting married is still much more than a legal formality.

I have done it, I realize. I have just married myself, in the most private of private ceremonies. Never have I seen myself in quite this way, as the person with whom I will spend the rest of my life, not only because I may be the only one around to do so, but because she is someone to love and to cherish, for better, for worse, for richer, for poorer, in sickness and in health. I close my eyes and reimagine the scene. *Just look at that woman in the pink dress, standing under those twinkle lights. I can't believe I get to spend the rest of my life with her.*

Who knows if this marriage will last; clearly, I don't have a perfect track record. But in this sacred space, what I am feeling toward myself is something I have only experienced in the sanctity of marriage: a sense of commitment, love, even grace.

The Weird Place

I ran into a woman at the local farmer's market, let's call her Phoebe. We met about twenty years ago, when our kids were in preschool together. We could have been friends, except for one thing—my raging jealousy.

Phoebe is perfect. She looks like one of those pretty doctors on a Shonda Rimes television series, only she actually is a doctor in real life. At school drop-off, Phoebe and her equally good-looking husband used to stand with their arms around each other's waists as they waved goodbye to their progeny. My spouse and I rotated drop-off, so my non-waving arm just hung at my side, like a loose shutter. In the sunlight, Phoebe's teeth actually sparkled, then and now.

"It's good to see you," I greeted Phoebe, shocked by the realization I actually wasn't faking it. "It's called just being nice," Helmut has explained to me on many occasions, when I ask how he can always be so sociable, not just with friends and acquaintances, but also in the way he is willing to exchanges hellos with strangers on the hiking trail, or linger at cash registers for a friendly chat, whereas I just want to get the hell out of Home Depot.

Phoebe and I asked after each other's kids, both of us equally flummoxed by how they had somehow grown into young adults. Her oldest was getting married! One of my girls was recently elected as a state representative for our Vermont district. How could this be? What was her platform?—*Let's help kids never have to throw out empty containers!* But no, that was the centerpiece of her campaign back in middle school, when she had a propensity for putting empty milk cartons back in the fridge. Now, both she and her sister were responsible adults, but that didn't mean they weren't still my babies.

As Phoebe and I chatted in the gentle June breeze, we were encircled by the happy bustle of the farmer's market, with dozens of stands selling locally produced veggies, meats, cheeses, and baked goods. Artisans displayed hand-crafted pottery, jewelry, herbal balms and potions, beeswax candles, and homespun wool. The scent of fresh plants and flowers mingled with the enticing aroma of grilled paninis and ethnic cuisine from the food vendors. At the epicenter of the market, a duo on fiddle and flute played lively folk songs. Enveloped in this wholesome, convivial atmosphere, I could almost forget that folk music really gets on my nerves.

"How have you been?" Phoebe asked me. "How's work?"

Maybe it's because I spend an inordinate amount of time with only myself or my cat for company, or maybe it's because I'm a nervous talker, but when people ask me a simple question, like—How have you been?—often my mouth goes off its meds. Which is how I found myself telling Phoebe not only all about my work life, but then segueing into myriad other topics, ultimately landing on the subject of *mukbang,* a South Korean trend that has made its way into the United States, in which you watch strangers eat enormous amounts of food.

"Did you know professional *mukbangers* on YouTube can make up to ten thousand dollars a month?" I asked Phoebe. "And that doesn't even include sponsorships from food and drink brands." Finally, after hearing the word *mukbanger* coming from my lips for the thousandth time, I managed to interrupt myself. "How are things going with you?"

"I'm not sure," Phoebe hesitated and I felt this sudden, anticipatory tingling that our chit chat was about to get real. Or at least more real than extreme-eating videos. "I'm in a bit of a weird place," Phoebe tucked a coil of honey-kissed hair behind her seashell-shaped ear. "Actually, I've been meaning to talk with you."

Me? She'd been meaning to talk with me? Through the years, mutual acquaintances had often told me that Phoebe and I should be friends. ("She's such a lovely person. You guys would get along great!") But that didn't happen, for whatever reasons. Yet now that she was in a "weird place" she felt compelled to seek me out as a confidante? This begged the question, if people had been telling me for years how Phoebe was such a lovely person, what exactly had they been telling her about me?

"What do you mean 'a weird place?'" I prodded. In truth, it was refreshing to see a chink in this woman's armor of perfect teeth.

"I switched jobs last year," she replied, which elicited a flashback to another one of our rare encounters, maybe a decade ago, when she had mentioned that she was in the process of going from being an internist to—wait for it—a cardiologist. This time, however, she had transitioned into another medical specialty, but her new role and hours were far less demanding. "I wanted more time so I could be free to do other things," she explained. "Only now I'm not sure what to do with that time."

"What sort of things do you like to do?" I asked. Thanks, once again, to mutual friends, I'd heard that a few years back Phoebe and her family had moved to a hobby farm outside town to grow veggies and raise chickens, so I knew that possibility for a new venture was already covered.

"Well, I just got my yoga teacher certification," Phoebe shrugged like this was no big deal, "but I know I don't want to teach yoga."

Why was I so *not* surprised by this latest accomplishment, and a clue as to why the lovely Phoebe and I had never become friends. One must know one's limitations, and what I know is that there is such a thing as too perfect a person for my insecurities to handle. Still, talking with her now, I barely registered a twinge of jealousy at Phoebe's latest accomplishment, despite the fact that jealousy, for me, is like shingles—always there, lying in wait in my nerve tissue, ready to reactivate at a moment's notice and set my torso on fire. But here at the farmer's market, instead of jealousy I felt kinship. For the first time I could actually relate to this woman; not to the internist-cardiologist-hobby-farmer-certified-yoga-teacher part, but the part about not being sure what to do with her free time.

"We should have coffee sometime soon," Phoebe suggested. "I'd like to pick your brain."

"That would be nice," I responded, once again surprised by my sincerity.

We said our goodbyes and continued separately making the rounds at the farmer's market, but our conversation lingered in my mind. *Why would Phoebe want to talk with me?* Maybe it was that she was considering taking one of my creative writing workshops now that she had more time on her hands. Or maybe she saw me as some kind of authority on weird places because of my unconventional career path, or simply because she thought I was weird though, compared to her, who wouldn't be weird? Regardless, I found it refreshing, even flattering, having something in my brain that Phoebe wanted to pick.

I stopped at a farmstand displaying rows of lettuce, radishes, peppers, and other produce. What truly was weird, I thought, was me contemplating buying lettuce that didn't come triple-washed in a bag. I bought a clump of freshly picked radishes, then moseyed over to the neighboring stand where I purchased a pretty plant. I could argue that when I was at the farmer's market I was in a weird place, given how it almost always managed to alleviate any grudgery I might feel toward the world, and brought out my inner Earth mother. Of course, once my inner Earth mother arrived back at her condo, we both knew she would give the pretty plant to her boyfriend, who would be the one to put it in the ground and nurture it to bloom.

As I continued to wander the market, Phoebe's comment kept looping in my mind—*I'm in a weird place.* It begged the question: What exactly qualified as *weird*? A memory resurfaced of watching one of those travel-adventure shows on TV, during which someone had made a comment to the effect, "Can you believe they eat guinea pigs here! This is such a weird place!" But is it weird? I thought at the time. Or is it just Peru?

In my own home state in America, one of the most prevalent slogans displayed on T-shirts, ballcaps, bottle openers, and baby onesies is "Keep Vermont Weird." Indeed, the slogan is so popular it has spawned a retail and online business entirely devoted to that mandate. But how weird can Vermont be, if a majority of the people here are wearing or carrying items bearing the same message? So, outside of Vermont, a state so determinedly and uniformly weird as to be almost normal, when was the last time I actually was in a weird place myself, either literally or metaphorically?

Norwegian Dawn.

Those were the first two words that popped into my head, and they fit the connotation of weirdness on every level, at least in my experience. *Norwegian Dawn* was the name of the 965-foot-long ship where, ten years prior, I had booked a seven-day cruise from Boston to Bermuda for me and my two daughters, then ages thirteen and fifteen, plus one of their friends. At this juncture in my life, the cruise was as much a mission as a vacation. It would be my first effort as a newly separated, solo mom to take my daughters on an adventure. I needed to prove I could do this, despite my inexperience as a traveler, my directional disability, and my learned helplessness. I figured a cruise would be a good starter vacation for someone like me because how wrong could things go? Essentially, we'd be confined to a 92,250-ton playhouse, with the exception of three days on the beaches of Bermuda. The only intimidating factor was the possibility of falling overboard, more likely a risk to me, which, as the responsible adult in our party, I greatly reduced by vowing that not a drop of alcohol would cross my lips for the entire duration of the cruise.

While the girls did their own thing for much of the days and evenings, my commitment was to make myself embrace every form of amusement this love boat had to offer. Dance parties! Gambling! Live theater and musical acts! Every night I put on a different party dress and left our cabin with the self-spoken directive, *You will have fun!* While another little voice in my head cruelly added, *And on this episode of Desperate Housewives . . .*

As a solo and sober cruiser, much of my time was spent eavesdropping on other people's conversations, which revealed that several of the 2,340 passengers on board the *Norwegian Dawn* were on their third, seventh, even tenth cruise! Socially, my fellow travelers seemed to configure and reconfigure as seamlessly as synchronized swimming float patterns, but apparently these *encruisiasts* (my word for all these gung-ho travelers) could spot a poseur like me faster than the spin of a one-armed bandit. No one reached out to me to join their parties, and I failed to insinuate myself into any conversations or cliques. Among the low points of the cruise was an afternoon spent playing trivia in the pub, where I found myself sitting solo, a team of one. A boisterous group crowded around the table beside mine. With my mind, I tried to will them to ask me to be on their team, but no such luck. My only comfort was that at the end of the competition I tied with them for the most correct answers, proving that my single brain knew as much trivia as all six of their beer-sodden noodles combined.

While I forced myself to look and act festive, I trusted that my girls and their friend were having real fun, though I suspect the cruise had to be a little bit of a weird place for them too. I recalled one afternoon when we all gathered for an afternoon cookout by the pool. The scene was wall-to-wall passengers on the upper and lower decks, most of them on the younger side. Upbeat music blared through the loudspeakers.

"Join the party!" A perky cruise employee greeted us, while manically handing out free pink slushies in hurricane glasses. My girls and I thanked her, filled our plates with food (so much good food on the cruise!), and managed to score some lounge chairs on the upper deck.

"Lay-deeze and dudes," the dance music was interrupted by a tan fellow in a muscle shirt and baggy swim shorts standing poolside and wielding a mic. "Slather on that sunscreen and get ready for a show!" He then put out a call to all the lovely lay-deeze in the audience to come join the wet T-shirt contest. (Let the record show that this was probably the only cruise activity in which I did not partake.) The MC went on to explain that the winner of the contest would be determined by whose nipples earned the loudest applause, or words to that effect.

As you might expect of Vermonters more accustomed to competitions where participants don ski parkas or decorate gingerbread houses, my fairly sheltered teenagers and I watched with wonderment as the bikini-clad volunteers happily donned white T-shirts and were then hosed down. I made a point to clap equally hard for each contestant, not wanting any of these young women to think that her soaking wet body wasn't worthy of appreciation. As a mother, I did enjoy an unexpected moment of pride during the event when I noticed my fifteen-year-old daughter looking a bit squeamish, which I chose to attribute to a burgeoning feminism, even though she'd been fighting seasickness for most of the cruise.

At the farmer's market, I made my last purchases—a loaf of freshly baked sourdough bread and a bottle of Vermont-made vodka. Rather than head home, however, I sat at one of the picnic tables scattered near the musicians and people-watched. I wondered, how many of these folks, like Phoebe, felt like they were in a weird place, for whatever reason? Probably a lot, I figured, given how often we find ourselves in transition, or in circumstances where we feel unsettled. We grow, we outgrow, and the next thing we know, we're back in unfamiliar territory.

It occurred to me that I also was in a weird place, given where I was at in my life, meaning somewhere between doing just fine and gone before you know it. Lately, I've caught myself thinking things that I'd never thought before, things like, *This will probably be the last dishwasher I ever have to buy.* Or, *I can't get a parrot because who will take care of it when I'm dead.* Yet at the same time, I still assumed I had all the time in the world. The other day I got an invitation to my high school class's fortieth reunion. Nah, I thought, I'll just wait and go to my next fortieth . . .

Watching all the people mingling around me, an idea took hold. I should set up my own booth at this farmer's market, maybe between the vendor selling jars of homemade jams covered with little gingham clothes and the stand occupied by an establishment called Lamb Farm that only sold organic beef patties.

My sign would read: "Consultant to People in Weird Places."

"Would it be accurate to say you're feeling adrift?" I imagined myself counseling anyone who stopped by to pick my brain. (Here, my previous experience on the cruise would come in handy.)

"Yes. Yes, that's the perfect way to describe it!" My new client would nod, adding, "I knew you would understand."

"No worries," I would continue in a comforting tone. "Everyone finds themselves in a weird place now and then, but I can promise you, you're probably going to be just fine!" This would not be an empty promise, because if my own experience on the *Norwegian Dawn* had taught me anything, it was that particular life lesson. Never had I felt so out of sorts, so lonely as I felt on that cruise. Yet, from the distance of a decade, I could now appreciate the value of that experience, far beyond the appeal of Bermuda's beaches, with sand as pink as the slushie in the hurricane glass that had been thrust into my eighth-grader's hand, and had turned out to be a strong margarita. Being in that particular weird place had put into relief how much I appreciated home and familiarity, even in the midst of a divorce. It also reinforced that I should never, ever consider moving to another town because, clearly, I had no idea how to make new friends.

I plucked a radish from my tote bag, brushed off some dirt, and took a bite. If I was a *mukbanger*, I thought, I could probably eat thousands of these little root vegetables at a single sitting, and make good money in the process. And if this reality wasn't proof positive that life itself was a weird place, I couldn't imagine what was. Plus, who was to say that things would be any different in the afterlife.

"I thought I wanted this," I envisioned clients like Phoebe coming all the way from heaven to avail themselves of my consulting services. "All those hours saving lives and doing yoga, but now, being stuck wearing a halo and hanging out with all these other divine souls, it just feels weird. To be honest, I'm bored as hell and not sure what to do with my time."

The folk duo in the center of the farmer's market launched into another lively tune, and some toddlers and adults wearing fanny packs started dancing in the grass. Here I was again, I realized, sitting alone among revelers, as I had often found myself on the *Norwegian Dawn*, only now I was feeling the opposite of lonely. The market bustled with a happy familiarity. People wanted to pick my brain. And, yes, given where I was at in my life, I understood all too well that I would be gone before I knew it, but at least there was comfort in knowing that I would never have to shell out for another dishwasher.

Keep Vermont weird. As if I needed proof that I was right where I belonged, I happened to look down, and there was my foot, tapping along to the music. How weird is that? I thought, given how, normally, folk music gets on my nerves.

The Real Reasons Writers Hate Amazon

Party Like It's 2044

Paperback — September 2023

By Joni B. Cole (Author)
2.5 stars ★★⯪ (13 ratings)

RedPen
★★ **Typo!**
(Reviewed in the United States on September 8, 2023)
Verified Purchase

Let this essay collection be a cautionary tale for other authors. You can write a 232-page book (73,661 words to be exact, minus the front matter, and yes, I did take the time to double check the word count), but you can't expect readers to take you or your work seriously when you either don't know how to spell the word "unforget-table," or you just don't care. Let these two stars serve as a reminder to this author, and anyone else who cares about proper spelling, the word unforgettable has two *t*s.

One person says, "Get a life."

GayleGayle

★ **Pet peeves**

(Reviewed in the United States on September 12, 2023)

Verified Purchase

Full disclosure, I took a writing workshop from Joni last year. First, she does NOT look like her author photo. Second, in every meeting the class would have to hear about her writing pet peeves. Like the word, *Suddenly.* ("There's nothing *sudden* about a three-syllable adverb!") And heaven forbid one of our characters *doubled over in laughter* or *shed a single tear.* (But then, I ask you, how do you let readers know when your character thinks something is hilarious or sad?) Truth be told, I didn't learn a thing in Joni's writing class and don't even know why I took it in the first place. (Why should I care about what other people have to say about *my* story?)

I did think this book of Joni's essays was okay overall, even though I was pretty sure I'd hate it. I can remember back when she was working on this collection and it sounded kind of ... weird when she talked about it, so I'm glad she managed to find a publisher. (Hope for us all!) I was going to give this book four stars to be nice, and I feel sorry for the author, but then I took away three of the stars because that's how many times Joni told me in class that I wasn't allowed to start my stories with a dream.

One person shed a single tear.

Joni B. Cole

★★★★★ **This is a satisfying book to review because I wrote it!**

(Reviewed in the United States on September 13, 2023)

Verified Purchase

Of course, *I* love this book. Why wouldn't I? I wrote it! And let me tell you, it's not easy to write a book, but boy-oh-boy everybody should do it. Like I always tell the aspiring authors in my own writing workshops, "Yes, your voice matters!" "Yes, everybody has stories worth sharing." "Yes, you can let go of that hurtful feedback from your writing professor thirty years ago—the one who told you that you lack *gravitas*. The man reeked of misogyny and some kind of pipe tobacco baked into his pretentious wool blazer. Plus, he creepy-flirted with some of the prettier women. So who cares that he made it clear through his dismissiveness and his single comment on your final project ("A few nice moments") that he thought you would never be a writer. Meanwhile, his latest release is a tour of brew pubs. (Gravitas, my ass!) To this prof I'd like to point out: I guess you were wrong, and I am a writer because otherwise how could I be sitting here leaving a review of My. Own. Book. I'd say that's reason enough to give myself five stars, if only to get your toxic feedback out of my head once and for all, you stupid shitbird!

One person found this cathartic.

Duane
★★★ **Male muddle**
(Reviewed in the United States on September 19, 2023)
Verified Purchase

This is a good book, but how did it get published when mine is just as good, and I can't ever get an agent to look at my manuscript? (In case you're interested, my book is entitled, *Male Muddle*, and is the moving story of a middle-aged product manager who finds his world upended when his new secretary turns out to be female, feisty, and out for his job!) I just don't get it. Just because I'm a white male, it seems like all of the sudden I'm the bad guy and out in the cold. It's not fair. I'm not even like those other white males, the ones you read about in the newspaper every day. I don't make sex jokes. I'm open-minded. My thirty-year-old boy, he tells me he's bisexual; I tell him I love him just the same. (But does he have to wear those kilts?) It seems like all anybody cares about these days, including publishers, are folks who are *marginalized*, to use my kid's word, or stories about zombies, or women who do crazy things like marry themselves. I'm not judging. People can marry whoever the heck they want. But I just don't get it. I really don't.

One person commented, "Hang in there. One day you'll get it."

MidgeandWalt
★★ **Nothing useful about Guatemala.**
(Reviewed in the United States on September 26, 2023)

I don't recommend this book and my husband doesn't either. We (almost) bought it because the first chapter looked like it was going to be about Guatemala, and our church group is going there on a two-week mission to do the Lord's work. We were hoping for travel tips. How do you stay safe in a Third World country? Will we need shots? (Nothing will convince us to get that vaccine with microchips!) Where are the best American restaurants? (My husband has dyspepsia and cannot tolerate spicy foods!) I only got so far as to read the book's first few paragraphs before I could tell right away this author has never even set foot in Guatemala. She should be ashamed of herself. I will pray for her, and my husband will too.

One person found nothing useful about this review.

WeedMan

★★★★★ **Read this book stoned.**

(Reviewed in the United States on October 2, 2023)

Verified Purchase

Man, this author chick is a trip. She writes letters to dead people and morphs into a talking kidney. She also talks to her cat and, get this, her cat talks back! I read this book and it blew my mind. I bet the author was on some good shit when she wrote it. I give it six stars. Maybe Joni could hook me up with her dealer?

One person commented, "The first step to recovery is to admit there is a problem."

Joni B. Cole

★★★★★ **Yet another person just asked, aren't you that author, Joni B. Cole? (Ugh, I knew I should've worn makeup today.)**

(Reviewed in the United States on October 3, 2023)

Verified Purchase

Feeling blessed (and wiped). My publicist just called (the poor woman is *besieged*) with yet another invite, this one for me to be "in conversation with" Elizabeth Gilbert!!! (Note to self: Don't fawn like you did when Tina Fey asked for a signed copy of your book at the Brooklyn Book Festival!) Oh, heads up LA pals! Heading your way soon to be keynoter at this, like, *mega* literary festival. (Gotta lose those icky three pounds to fit in that size zero!) Nervous as H-E-double toothpicks because Zadie (as in Zadie Smith, y'all) was last year's keynoter. (Doesn't that word look funny when you write it: *key*noter, key*noter*, *keynoter*.) Anyhoo, Zades told me I got this! Gratitude. 🙏 for BFFs. Now I just need to remember to put on my face when I go to Piloxing class. Ugh. Miss the days when I could just hide in the back without so many people knowing I'm famous. ☹

One person commented, "Hey, author, look up the word humble-brag and see your picture."

My Son is an Honor Student
⭐ **Never be friends with this author.**
(Reviewed in the United States on October 15, 2023)
Verified Purchase

Some writers should respect other people's privacy. (Remember, Joni, how I told you about my Aunt Vivian and then you put her in one of your "funny" little essays. Well she *died* last week. I hope you're happy!) *Some* writers should also stop twisting people's words and putting them in their characters' mouths. (I never said, "State schools are for losers." I simply said it was a shame Lily's daughter didn't get into Stanford like my Ethan.) And *some* writers—especially if you thought they were your *friend*—should think twice before writing about how they saw you at McDonald's, "wolfing down" fries and a shake. (And, no, it wasn't enough to simply change my name in the story because everyone knows I drive a silver Volvo wagon with a "My Son is an Honor Student" bumper sticker.) But here's what really hurts, Joni B. Cole. You didn't even thank me in your acknowledgments.

One person would like to express her condolences about Aunt Vivian.

JustKillMeNow

★ **Uh, hello. The world is on fire.**

(Reviewed in the United States on October 19, 2023)

Verified Purchase

Consider this one star a freebie because the author's writing is serviceable, but *really*? One of these essays is about "lambies in jammies." Another is about taking a Zumba class. Meanwhile, the human race is on the verge of World War III. If the nukes don't destroy everyone and everything on the planet then climate change will, or another mutant virus, or the plague of social media, or smartphones and all that blue light, or movie theater popcorn, or anti-bacterial soap, or dog saliva, or sitting ...

One person needs a hug.

Joni B. Cole

★★★★★ **This is the best lash grower I've ever tried.**

(Reviewed in the United States on October 27, 2023)

Verified Purchase

I've been applying Miracle-Lash every night for four weeks and I LOVE the results! Normally my lashes are stubby, but now they look like spider legs they're so long and curly. Plus, Miracle-Lash is safe for sensitive eyes. And one tube lasts a long, long time. (Oops, I just realized, this review was meant for another product. Oh well, five stars are five stars!)

One person loves the way her eyes pcp now that her lashes are so long and thick.

Regular Joe

★★★★ **Don't call it women's fiction.**

(Reviewed in the United States on November 18, 2023)

Verified Purchase

I thought you were supposed to call books like this *women's fiction*, where ladies write about their feelings. But my wife, Tillie, she doesn't like it when I say that. "You don't see a section called 'Men's Fiction,' she teased me, last time I drove her to the bookstore. (Tillie doesn't drive no more, not since the cancer came back.) Tillie also says this book isn't fiction. What do I know? I like John Wayne movies. But Tillie really liked this book, and since she says it's not women's fiction, I don't argue. Tillie's the boss and has been ever since we met back in grammar school.

Tillie gives this book four stars. "Why not five?" I asked, when I finished reading her the last story. (Tillie can't see so good anymore, so now I'm the reader in the family.) "Because you're the only thing that deserves five out of five stars," she said and gave me a peck. It still confounds me. How did a regular Joe like me end up with someone so pretty and smart as Tillie? Come next January, it'll be sixty years she's put up with me and John Wayne. Hang on, sweetheart. There's lots more books I need to read.

One person is thinking about her grandparents.

★★★★★ **Bird by bird**

(Reviewed in the United States on November 19, 2023)

I've taken a ton of Joni's writing workshops and I think she's a really good teacher. (She's so nice!) I know she wrote another book before this one that was about writing. (*Write Naked* or something like that?) I didn't read it, but I did read Anne Lamott's book on writing, *Bird by Bird*, and if you're an aspiring author like me, you have to get that book! It's amazing. It's the best writing guide ever! I tell everyone in Joni's workshops, *Bird by Bird* is the only writing book they'll ever need. Anyway, when this new book of Joni's came out, she asked everyone in our group to write a review so here's mine. Five stars for *Bird by Bird*!

One person is not as nice as some of her students think.

Nana

★ **Did I do this right?**

(Reviewed in the United States on November 21, 2023)

This is my first Amazon review. Well, I wrote a review last Christmas about my InstaPot, but that review didn't work. I think I forgot to press the right button. (The InstaPot was such a thoughtful gift from my granddaughter, but I still like my pressure cooker better.) I got this book by Joni B. Cole from one of those little free libraries shaped like bird houses. (Nowadays, you see those cute bird houses everywhere. It's so nice how you never have to buy books anymore!) I think this author is clever as the dickens and some of her stories will have you chuckling, so I'm happy to give this book a star!

One person hates those little free libraries.

MagicCandle
★★★★★ **Psychic fail**
(Reviewed in the United States on November 30, 2023)
Verified Purchase

I went to an astrologist I've never seen before to read my
sex horoscope, and she told me these next few months
were the perfect time to prioritize my pleasure, express
my desires, and try something new! Right before I left
this lady's house (she does readings out of her kitchen), I
noticed she had this book by Joni B. Cole on her counter.
So I figured it was a sign, and I bought myself a copy.
Three weeks later, my boyfriend, Shawn, broke up with
me and now my sex life is in retrograde. If this astrolo-
ger's taste in writers is as sucky as her psychic powers, I
don't see much point in reading this book. I'm still giving
it five stars though because, well, you know, Karma. But if
anyone wants my copy, I'm selling it on eBay for 99 cents.

One person agrees, what goes around comes around.

Joni B. Cole
★★★★★ **Can't wait for my next book!**
(Reviewed in the United States on December 3, 2023)
Verified Purchase

I've said it before and I'll say it again, "Yes, your voice
matters!" "Yes, everybody has stories worth sharing." The
time has come for me to start writing a brand-new book,
just as soon as I finish the eleven new series on Netflix.
In the meantime, everybody, please, please, please buy
this book! Buy it for yourself and your family! Buy it for
your friends and frenemies. Buy it even if you have to
purchase it from Amazon, the evilest of evil corporations

and destroyer of independent booksellers and local economies (though it's still better than those little free libraries)! And when you do buy your copy (or copies!) of this book from Amazon or wherever books are sold, don't forget to leave a review!

One person commented, "On second thought, maybe skip the review if you're not a fan."

The Age of Authenticity

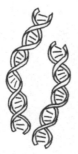

"You know what I like about you," the woman seated next to me at the conference leaned over and confided, "I can tell you're courageously yourself."

"Thank you," I said, assuming her compliment was prompted by the keynote address I'd given that morning to this group of a hundred or so women business owners. But then I thought, Wait a minute. Is that really a compliment? Why would she think it took courage to be me?

I'd barely met this person, but like I often do, I'd already imagined her life story—a can-do entrepreneur determined to make the most of her empty nest. She starts every day with a feminist quote and a to-do list, and every other Sunday she meets her gal pals for brunch at their reserved table. Actually, this Brunch Lady shared a similar vibe with most of the people I'd met at the conference. A good many of them, so it seemed, worked as life coaches. These were exactly the kind of organized, go-getter women I both admired and resented every time I saw them gathered at busy restaurants, laughing and raising their mimosas in toasts, while I fumed at the hostess stand after being told there'd be a three-hour wait.

During the morning of the conference, I'd delivered a talk on the subject of "Finding Gratitude in Unexpected Places." Gratitude was the theme of this day-long event, so I'd shared some professional failures and how they'd had surprising upsides. One example was the time I'd been scheduled to do a reading from my first collection of essays. For some reason, the manager of the bookstore where I was to present had set me up in the children's section, even though my book was for adults. As the start of the event came and went, all the seats remained empty until, finally, a woman settled herself in one of the vacant rows. There, she proceeded to read aloud *A Bear Called Paddington* to her two toddlers. My own kids used to love Paddington when they were little, so it was nice hearing the book read aloud and recalling those memories. Mostly, however, the upside of this experience was that it helped toughen me up for a host of similar humiliations that followed at subsequent readings.

At the conference, I had wanted to ask the Brunch Lady seated next to me to elaborate—*Why did she think it took courage to be me?* But then the afternoon speaker took the stage. This presenter was about fifty, with short curly hair and enviable biceps. She wore one of those wireless microphone headsets that I always associate with rock stars. Before my own talk, the conference organizers had asked me if I wanted a similar headset, but I declined, given my presentation style is to stay immobilized behind the podium and read from a script, while trying to pretend that I'm not reading from a script. The afternoon speaker's presentation was entitled, "Respite," and as she spoke she roamed the stage, backlit by a series of inspirational quotes projected onto a super-sized screen. At artful interludes her voice undulated from commanding to hushed, depending on the point she was making. She seemed to make eye contact with every listener, her gaze as taut as her biceps. Even the woman's strategic silences reverberated through the room, demanding we pause for reflection.

My gosh, this woman was a masterful speaker, I thought, though another small part of me was also thinking, this whole TedX thing has really gotten away from us.

In the weeks following the conference, I kept revisiting the Brunch Lady's comment to me—"*I can tell you're courageously yourself.*" But how? I wondered. How exactly was I courageously myself? Maybe I was missing something, but I really didn't think it took all that much courage to be me. For starters, I was born a female and identify as female, so no heroics there. In addition, I live in Vermont, a state overrun with bleeding-heart liberals much like myself, so if ever I found myself, say, advocating for free school lunches and affirmative action during town meeting, I really didn't have to worry about a fur-wearing woman seated next to me indignantly responding, *"I don't believe in entitlement programs!"* I also didn't earn my living through a normal office job, so there was no need to bravely assert my preference to dress like a slob, or confront HR about needing to bring my "service animal" (aka Kitty) to the office for my well being. In fact, given all the graces and latitude in my life that allowed me to be so thoroughly myself, this helped explain why often I purposely assumed different personas, if only as a way to switch things up a bit.

"Who are you supposed to be now? "Helmut had asked me the other evening when he came downstairs and found me swooning against the couch. In this scenario, I was a Victorian Housewife, stricken with the vapors. "Could I trouble you to bring me a snifter of sherry?" I requested in a weakened voice. "Not that glass, dear," I gently chided him, hand to bosom, intimating the possibility of consumption. "The *larger* snifter, if you please." Delicate cough, cough, cough.

Other times and in other moods, I have played the part of Independent Woman, assuming a wide stance, arms akimbo—"No one puts Joni in a corner!" Or, I have embodied the role of the Busy Professional—"You want me to pick up my dirty clothes from the floor? Ask someone who isn't under deadline!" These characters and a host of others all resided in me, along with new personalities frequently popping up to suit an occasion or a whim.

If there was one thing that I took away from that conference rich in life coaches (aside from a lovely glass paperweight), it was a reminder of the importance of being an authentic person. Being an authentic person means being true to who you really are deep down. It means pursuing your passions and listening to that inner voice guiding you forward. It means speaking your opinions honestly to the world. To paraphrase the psychologist-slash-superstar Brené Brown (who was quoted so many times at the conference she might as well have been given a box lunch)—authenticity is an essential part of developing meaningful relationships. "In order for connection to happen," she espouses, "we have to allow ourselves to be seen, really seen."

Authenticity. It's a meaningful goal. Plus, who would be stupid enough to argue with Brené Brown? No one, it seems, given the term "authenticity" has become a buzzword, a part of the zeitgeist of the modern age.

"I love this rose shimmer blush." I recently heard some influencer gush while sharing her morning makeup routine on her Instagram reel. "It gives you that authentic, no-makeup glow, so you can look like you, only better."

I wasn't sure how rose shimmer blush on your cheekbones accentuated your authentic self, but I do understand why it's important to remind people, especially women, to be true to themselves. Let's face it, the centuries-old doctrine of coverture (a legal practice in English common law that basically denied women an identity) may have been disassembled in the nineteenth century, but its traces are still visible in modern laws and politics. Plus, even if some outside oppressor isn't trying to tell us what to do with our lives and our bodies, it still can be hard to honor our authentic selves because . . . well just because it's hard.

I thought about my friend Bianca, the nicest woman on the planet, even to her boyfriend, whom she has been fed up with for over twenty years. The boyfriend is not the worst guy in the world; he just never wants to do anything that doesn't involve a screen, and his idea of a compliment is something like, "These meatballs aren't as good as the ones you made last week." I suspect Bianca's unhappy relationship might help explain her habit of walking into a room, any room, and immediately apologizing.

"Sorry. Have you seen my car keys?"

"Sorry, but you might be interested in this article I just read."

"Sorry. I'm going to the movies. Do you want to come along?"

It's hard to believe that Bianca really believes she should apologize for inviting someone to the movies, so I have to think something else is going on inside her head, like maybe her inauthentic self feels the need to constantly apologize to her authentic self—*Sorry you're still with that lardass!*

With my own boyfriend, Helmut, if either of us were to be labeled the lardass in our relationship that would be me, proof that I was indeed courageously myself, and had no trouble letting my authenticity all hang out. But this brought to mind a different question—*Was being your authentic self always a good thing?* In this Age of Authenticity, just raising the question might make you suspect, but what if your authentic self wasn't always someone whom others wanted to be around?

Me, yesterday at the bakery: *I don't give a shit if you're short-staffed. And maybe if you didn't chat up every customer, asking about where they got their nails done, I'd get my Americano without having to wait in line for twelve hours. And next time, fill my coffee cup to the top, as in all the way to the brim. How many times do I have to tell you people: No. Room. For. Cream!*

No, I didn't say any of that aloud, preferring to just allow the barista to read my scowl, but regardless, those thoughts were part of my authentic self, at least in that moment. And if I was being even more brutally authentic, I could list countless other examples of my bad behavior and nasty thoughts, also true to the real me. Like when I kicked the printer after it jammed. Or willfully lingered a half hour after the bookstore's closing time, even while the manager vacuumed under my feet. Or when I berated the Verizon customer service rep in that little online chat box because I hate those little chat boxes. Or how I wished, really wished, that I could just thrice click my salt and pepper shakers—click, click, click—and magically manifest a plague of locusts around Mar-a-Lago.

These examples made the argument that maybe it made sense to curb my authentic self, at least some of the time. Plus, there had been other indications that being myself didn't always prove the best role model. On Mother's Day a few years ago, for example, my daughter had sent me a card on which she had written, *I'm glad I am growing up to be like you.* What beautiful words—all the work of raising a child paid off in that one daughterly sentiment. But then that sentence was followed by this: *I'll try to make you proud by winning a bunch of liability lawsuits.* I have never sued anyone in my life, but my daughter's humor did capture my proclivity to want to make people pay for all the wrongs I have suffered, real or imagined.

Who do you think you are?!

How dare you inconvenience me like this!

I demand to speak to the manager!

For years, I have resisted using those DNA testing services that promise to "tell you who you really are" by revealing your ancestry and genetic data. My aversion to these tests used to be because I never wanted to find out if I was part Neanderthal, which just seems embarrassing, even though it's not all that uncommon. But now I had even more reason to avoid confronting a breakdown of my identity:

Joni B. Cole
32 percent European Jewish
29 percent Ireland/Scotland/Wales
3 percent Neanderthal
9 percent plague-of-locusts advocate
27 percent *that person*

I could just imagine this representation of my genome, a composite of the good, the bad, and the obnoxious. In this way we are all related, I thought, given that everyone has a few pathogenic variants, even if those unfortunate genes are more recessive in some folks than others. Suddenly, it made sense, this surge of incivility we've been experiencing in the world—people yelling and screaming at each other across the aisle; travelers berating airline personnel because they aren't allowed to take their Big Gulps on the plane; anti-vaxxers sending death threats to scientists who are probably looking at each other at their NIH conferences, thinking, *What the hay? We're just a bunch of molecular biologists.*

Welcome to the Age of Authenticity! where we all are encouraged to embrace our true selves, even when it makes us think and act like Neanderthals.

When I look back on that conference for women business owners, I'm still not sure why Brunch Lady felt compelled to call me courageous just for being myself. My best guess is that it had to do with my willingness to share some of my professional low points, though if I had really been fully authentic, I would have shared some additional details, including the fact that whenever I fail, a part of me wants to cry, give up, and lash out at anyone and everything.

"Fuck Paddington the bear!" That's what I wanted to scream at that mother who was reading aloud to her two toddlers at my author event, ridiculously relegated to the children's section of the bookstore. "My book is for adults! I'm an adult! Get those little brats out of here!"

But I didn't yell any of those things. Instead, I managed to suppress my natural instincts, smile politely, and hide my authentic self. And for that I was grateful, unexpectedly so, and even a little proud. Because for all this talk about listening to our inner voice, speaking our truth, and being who we really are deep down, I think sometimes it takes more courage to *not* be ourselves. Or at least not be the 27 percent of our true natures that makes us *that person*.

Social Grooming

When my younger daughter was in middle school and in her button phase—meaning her school backpack was covered with pins bearing pithy comments like "Furious George' and "Please don't interrupt me while I'm ignoring you," I found one for her that I was sure she would love. It was oversized and bright pink with bold lettering that read: "I Just Love to Make New Friends!"

"No thank you," she said, handing it back to me.

In hindsight, I can see now how the sentiment probably didn't jibe with middle school humor, or maybe it hit too close to home in terms of teenage insecurities, but, to quote from a pin my daughter actually felt worthy of her backpack, "Whatever." I thought the pin I'd bought was hilarious and promptly attached it to the strap of my shoulder bag. Long gone were my own button-collecting days, but sometimes you just do things to crack yourself up, or to show your kids that you're not the least bit hurt by their rejection.

Fast forward a few hours on that same day, when I found myself skulking near the hostess stand of a busy restaurant, waiting to meet a colleague named Shannon. At work, Shannon, a graphic designer, seemed fun, like someone you could actually envision as a real person outside the office—someone who might cannonball into a swimming pool, for example, shouting, "Cowabunga!" So you hear yourself saying spontaneous, non-work-related things to her like "We should meet up for dinner sometime!" But eventually, after you've tossed out this suggestion a certain amount of times without following through with an actual plan, it gets embarrassing and becomes another one of those items weighing on your mental to-do list, along with getting your tire pressure checked, or writing a sympathy card to your neighbor whose mother died two years ago, or replacing the box of K-Cups you stole from your ex's house last Thanksgiving. *Follow-up with graphic designer Shannon about dinner!!!*

So, finally, I had indeed followed through and we'd set a date and time to meet at this restaurant, but now where the hell was Shannon? As diners came and went, I squeezed to the side of the crowded entrance and stood sentinel, given the restaurant's policy that all parties must be present to be seated. Who thought of that policy, anyway? The Shamers' Society? I rechecked the exchange of previous texts between Shannon and me, to make sure I hadn't mixed up the details of our rendezvous, and wrote her again:

> Waiting at the front of the restaurant. Looking forward to seeing you. ☺

By now she was a half hour late. Maybe I should have told the hostess I was dining alone so that she would have seated me, and then act surprised if Shannon had actually appeared—*"Oh my gosh, what are you doing here?!"* Finally, I conceded Shannon had either forgotten about our dinner, or stood me up. "My friend must have mixed up the date," I told the hostess on my way out the door. "She can be such a scatterbrain," I added, but what I was really thinking was, *Shannon, you cannonballing cowabunga . . .*

"Have a nice rest of your evening," the hostess responded, crossing my name off her list.

Back in the car, I tossed my purse on the passenger seat, and that's when I realized just how pathetic I must have looked to all those other diners coming and going. I could just imagine what they were thinking as they passed by me: *How sad, that poor woman standing all alone. Look at how she watches the door, such an eager smile plastered on her face. And what's written on that big pink pin on her shoulder bag? Something about how she loves to make new friends. Oh, that poor, desperate creature.*

Social scientists have long touted the importance of friendship; how connection is not just a cultural but a biological need, and how the strength of our social bonds factor into our very survival. Some of this knowledge is owed to a much-observed baboon in Botswana named Sylvia, aka the Queen of Mean, because of her clear disdain for the other females in her troop. For years, Sylvia only deigned to do social grooming with her daughter, Sierra, but then Sierra got eaten by a lion. After that, poor Sylvia became so depressed that she stopped being so mean and began grooming one of the other females she had previously considered beneath her, demonstrating that such is our need for social bonding that we're willing to pluck hard-to-reach ticks and insects from just about anyone, as long as they'll call us friend.

In high school, I was a lot like Sylvia. That is, I had exactly one friend, and felt lucky to have that many, though in my case it was social anxiety, not disdain, that dissuaded me from reaching out to other females, or any person for that matter. Also similar to Sylvia's story, I ended up losing that friend—renamed Lauren here, for the sake of discretion—not because Lauren was eaten by a lion, but rather because she started dating a boy from a private school our junior year and abruptly stopped hanging out with me. Of course, I thought with bitterness at the time, it was inevitable that Lauren, star of the floor exercises event on the gymnastics team, would never settle for a public school boyfriend. Though, to be fair, our high school was overrun with Mennonites, which didn't exactly ignite the libido, at least when you're a sixteen-year-old girl.

From childhood into my thirties—this was how my social life proceeded, with me having, on average, one friend at a time. But then that friend would move out of town, or get too busy to see me after their third child, or ghost me, or die and break my heart. These losses felt like, not just blows, but betrayals. *Thanks a lot! Now who am I going to hang out with on Friday nights?* Meanwhile, the social scientists—who had already made it clear that our very survival depended on being popular—also made it sound like the chances of making new friends once you reached adulthood were virtually nil. Apparently, the average adult spends just forty-one minutes a day socializing, yet it typically takes more than two hundred hours, ideally over six weeks, for a stranger to grow into a close friend. Two-hundred hours! Who has that kind of time and energy?

As it turns out, I did. Or rather, I did once I started the Writer's Center of White River Junction, Vermont, located in a downtown building aptly named Dreamland. My writer's center was just a single room with orange walls, just big enough to accommodate a circle of mismatched furniture and a minifridge. When I established the center, my original intention was to have my own space to teach creative writing to adults in my community, but I quickly discovered an ulterior benefit. Week after week, workshop after workshop, the writer's center created the perfect opportunity to lure diverse and interesting people right to my door, where I would then audition them for the role of friend, whether they knew it or not.

Did this person make me laugh? Check.

Did they dislike dogs? Uncheck.

Were they slightly weird? Check?

Did they believe in fairies? Uncheck.

Conveniently, the majority of my classes ran for six weeks—apparently, the necessary span of time for friend-making—and while we didn't have two hundred hours together over the course of a single workshop, most of the participants signed on for concurrent sessions, or returned intermittently through the years. It also helped that a writing workshop is like a hothouse environment; if it feels supportive—like we're all in it together, laying bare our creative efforts—this atmosphere accelerates intimacy and bonding. To make sure everyone brought their better self to class, I'd hung a sign on the wall: Non-Judgment Day is Here!

Because I felt so at home at the writer's center, it gave me a confidence that I typically lacked in the outside world. As such, it was not uncommon for me to make the first friendly overture, once I determined whether a candidate was ready for the next stage of bonding. I might toss out something like, "Let's grab a drink after the workshop!" Or, "Come to my Galentine's Day party!" Even nicer, sometimes the friend candidate, perhaps sensing the same compatibility I was feeling, would be the one to take the initiative. For example, a woman named Janna, a painter about my age, once asked me to go with her to a performance-art workshop on a Saturday afternoon. There, we had to dress up as creatures called Poofs, our costumes best described as six-foot-tall cocoons made of hoops and covered in tulle, with no eye holes. Embedded inside these puppet creatures, sightless and forced to breathe in our own stale air, we learned how to writhe in ways that expressed different emotions. The class culminated in us having to writhe in a public space (in our case a popular ice cream shop) while trying to engage bystanders.

Would I ever go to a performance-art workshop again? Uncheck.

Despite the nightmare of it all, did I appreciate the way Janna did her best to emote displeasure when a child with a cone tried to touch her tulle? Check.

And with that, I added another good friend to my ever-widening social circle, cultivated over twenty years of running in-person classes at the Writer's Center of White River Junction, Vermont.

March 2020. When COVID took hold, I abruptly stopped all workshops at the writer's center, but, like so many others, I failed to fathom the reality of the situation. "See you in a few weeks," I said, not only to my workshop participants but to the protagonists and narrators I liked to think hid behind the orange walls, and between the couch cushions, and in the cracks in the old leather recliner that had once been my father's favorite chair before this space inherited it. By now there must have been thousands of characters dwelling in this room. Left to their own devices, I imagined what they did after their authors went home: The ones from the literary works would be the first to grab the wine bottles from the minifridge. The crime novel murderers and their victims would practice swing dancing together. And the narrators of their memoirs would happily hang out with their moms and dads, even though they never seemed to get along on the pages. With the real world so divided, I wanted the warm bubble of the writer's center to extend to everyone, even the characters who were created there.

After the worst of the pandemic, when I re-entered this space for the first time in months, everything felt unfamiliar, cold. I took a seat in the green velvet chair with the sagging seat cushion. For too many workshops to count, this was the chair where a fellow named Mike always sat, making a point to arrive early to class just so that no one else could lay claim to it. The group of us who were part of that friend circle still called this "Mike's Chair" for years, even after he'd died.

I looked around the center at the shabby furniture. The fridge was still covered with a nonsensical arrangement of magnetic poetry. The sheen on the orange walls seemed to have lost its luster. It occurred to me that, if I'd forgotten to toss the last filter we'd used in the coffeemaker, the grounds must be as desiccated as a fossil.

Well after the arrival of vaccines and the end of the official lockdown, I still had avoided returning to my writer's center, and my first foray back reinforced why. During the pandemic, I had been teaching solely online, where a lot of familiar faces I'd previously seen week after week had been replaced by Zoom participants from all over the country, even overseas. Why someone from Maui, or Copenhagen, or Texas would take workshops through a place called the Writer's Center of White River Junction, Vermont, remained a mystery to me, but I was as grateful as I was surprised. Now, it was hard to come back to this room. Over the months of my absence, it felt like I had moved on, like I'd outgrown the limitations of this small physical space. So what was I to do?

"We know you're not coming back here to teach anymore." I could hear all those protagonists and narrators whispering from their hiding places. "You're going to abandon us after all these years, and then we'll all be evicted!" Of course, they were simply echoing what I'd already been thinking. Months ago I had realized that it no longer made sense to continue to rent a physical space, not when my online classes and other opportunities were bringing in more work than I could handle. Still, I hadn't been certain what I was going to do until I returned. One look around the writer's center made my decision inevitable. The specter of the pandemic still lingered, and our tight circle of chairs left little room for social distancing. But then again, I thought, already feeling the loss, hadn't that closeness always been one of the best things about my little space?

The first time I returned to my writer's center was also the first time I'd set foot in downtown White River Junction in months. Maybe it was the pall of the pandemic, mixed with being holed up in my house for so long, but I think I'd expected to find the equivalent of Pompeii, a relic of an ancient time, preserved under ash and pumice. It surprised me how the people I remembered from the before-days still existed, for the most part their stores and cafés intact. In the long stretch away, I felt like I had lost the ability to converse face to face, even with people I used to see all the time. "Hello. How. Are. You? I. Am. Fine. Goodbye." This setback in my social skills was hardly a surprise. During the pandemic, I had barely groomed myself, let alone others.

Still, I almost hate to admit this, but those months of lockdown and isolation had an upside for me. The reset did me good, allowing me time to hunker inward, rethink how I teach, concentrate on my own writing projects, and dial back what was often a too hectic pace of life. But now that things have returned to some kind of new normal, the time has come to focus outward, open up my world, and rebuild my much-depleted social circle. It hasn't proven easy. Without the use of my writer's center to provide a steady stream of friend candidates, I've been forced to look further afield.

> Was that woman I met for coffee at the diner warm and outgoing? Check.

> Would I want to hear more about her dietary restrictions? Uncheck.

> Do I still have Shannon's contact info? Check.

> Do I still cringe whenever I think of how I must have looked standing at the entrance of that restaurant, sporting that oversized pink pin? Uncheck.

I know if I'm going to succeed at rebuilding my friend circle, the key will be to keep an open mind and, even more important, an open heart, which doesn't always come easy to me. But if Sylvia the baboon has taught me anything, it's that one is not enough, at least when it comes to social grooming. I don't want to find myself in Sylvia's predicament, alone and lonely down the road, covered with ticks and insects. So many bonds were broken during the pandemic, but as any social scientist can tell you, having strong connections with others is not just a luxury, it's a matter of survival. And like anything that matters, you just have to put in the time, say two hundred hours, and the next thing you know a stranger turns into a friend.

Appreciations

Traditionally, this part of the book is entitled "Acknowledgments," but something about that word, at least for this collection, didn't feel right. For one thing, the word's definition—"an author's statement of indebtedness"—connotes a formality that doesn't fit with my mindset, which is that I wish I could just skip all convention and hug every person who kept me writing or sane. It also occurred to me, on the rare occasions when I do use that word, I'm usually not at my best, as in, "I acknowledge that I ate the last piece of cake, but *you* finished the milk and then put the empty carton back in the fridge!"

All this to say, I "acknowledge" I may have unresolved issues, but what I really want to communicate here is how much I truly appreciate the individuals listed below:

To Helmut Baer, who contributed all the illustrations to this collection. I love you, but that is only one of the many reasons why.

To my girls, Esme and Thea, and their dad Steve, who lived several of these stories with me. The Cole family endures with love and laughter! I look forward to more family dinners and holiday gatherings, especially now that (most) of the kitchen appliances are working.

To Marjorie Matthews, one of the most thoughtful and generous people in the universe, right down to her willingness to listen to (and laugh at) my rants. Marjorie proved a discerning first reader for most of the essays in this collection, but even when her only comment was, "I love it," she somehow inspired me to tackle another draft. Or seven. I can't imagine how I would have plowed through the writing process without her insights, cheerleading, and all-around wonderfulness.

To Deb McKew, whom I got to know and befriend in the *before* days—when I was the editor and she was the intern. My, how our roles have reversed! I want to publicly apologize to Deb for making her fall behind on her own book deadline because she was so busy offering me feedback and correcting the grammar and punctuation in this book. My hope is that a fancy home-cooked dinner (Helmut's cooking, of course) will help make it up to her.

To Ed Ting, who is ridiculously gifted at too many things—writing, astronomy, piano, and especially friendship. Ed also is a freakishly good proofreader who actually read this book in manuscript form and noticed that one of the spaces between two words was erroneously in italics. *Who does that?*

To Herb Prem, my beloved "patron," who keeps telling me I should focus on the funny. He's right, of course, because the funny is what always brings me back to writing, even if I don't stay there for long. Herb and I met when he emailed me several years ago asking for my editorial assistance with a project. At some point, he started calling me his "muse," which basically means that I keep badgering him to send me more of his brilliant and timeless short stories.

To Elise McHugh, my editor at University of New Mexico Press, who provided immeasurable guidance during our weekly Thursday afternoon meetings. As much as I appreciated all those check-ins, I also appreciated the time Elise canceled on me, but sent the following note: *If you want to meet though or feel it's important that we do so, please let me know! I don't want you to think you're not a priority, because you absolutely are!* ☺ No editor has ever made me feel more like a priority, let alone put it in writing.

And, finally, to all the big-hearted people in my writing workshops and social circles past, present, and let's hope in the future. Without the sustenance of meaningful work, shared stories, and friendship, I know I would be as sad and nasty as Sylvia the baboon and would probably never leave my house.

About the Author

Joni B. Cole is the author of seven books, including two writing guides: *Good Naked: How to Write More, Write Better, and Be Happier, Revised and Expanded Edition* (listed as one of the "Best Books for Writers" by *Poets & Writers Magazine*); and *Toxic Feedback: Helping Writers Survive and Thrive, Revised and Expanded Edition* ("I can't imagine a better guide to writing's rewards and perils than this fine book"—*American Book Review*). She is a teacher and speaker at a variety of academic programs, writing conferences, and nonprofit organizations. Joni is also the creator and host of the podcast *Author, Can I Ask You?* and a contributor to *The Writer* magazine. *Party Like It's 2044* is her second collection of personal essays. Joni lives in Vermont. For more information, visit www.jonibcole.com.